Becoming Mother Martha

Through adversities comes greatness.

Based on True Events.

Martha Hoy

Copyright © 2022 by Martha Hoy

All rights reserved

This book is dedicated to King Edward Mutesa, the first President of Uganda and King of the Buganda Kingdom. Like me, he was exiled from his home but died in exile. I ran for my life with just a suitcase from my home in West Virginia in 2018. Because my Ugandan family was there for me, I lived to tell my story. Thank you, Ivan and Joe, for ensuring my safety in Minnesota. To Sam for becoming like the brother I never had. For showing me how a man should treat a woman and for welcoming me into your family. To Daniel for always being my camera man, and for all the laughs we have had together. Geofrey, my sponsor child, my heart on two legs. I am eternally grateful for all my Ugandan family.

Contents

Introduction... vii

Chapter 1: Overcoming Hardships: The catalysts that changed my life. 1

Chapter 2: The Recovery.. 11

Chapter 3: My life as a nurse with a lot of replacement parts. 17

Chapter 4: Life without connection brings loneliness. 19

Chapter 5: A connection was found in an unexpected place. 21

Chapter 6: I had a realization that changed everything. 27

Chapter 7: She's on the run.. 31

Chapter 8: Healing in Minnesota begins and a new family emerges. 37

Chapter 9: Viva Las Vegas.. 43

Chapter 10: Journey around the world. 47

Chapter 11: A new Family Emerges.. 49

Chapter 12: Welcome to the Pearl of Africa.. 55

Chapter 13: Visiting Bulamu where Geofrey grew up was a real eye opener. 67

Chapter 14: A date with a Prince. 75

Chapter 15: Then there was danger. 87

Chapter 16: A date with a Prince, Pizza in Milan and
           a plane trip home.. 95

Chapter 17: 2020 the year of the nurse. A pandemic nurse
           in a tourist town. 99

Chapter 18: A weekend in Vegas with a Prince. 109

Chapter 19: Surviving Covid.. 115

Chapter 20: Take me home country roads.. 119

Introduction

This is my story, how I went from being a nurse West Virginia to becoming known as Mother Martha in Uganda. I was an abused, shell of a person, at the end of a journey of self-discovery, I was known as a leader and an advocate for children over 7,000 miles away, in an East African country. I wrote it in such a way that it feels like you and I, the reader, are sitting on the front porch together and I am telling you this story.

I hope listening to my story inspires you, teaches you something or puts a smile on your face. That it gives you hope during times of adversity and opens your heart and mind to people in different parts of the world.

Thank you for spending this time with me.

Much love to you my friends,

Martha Hoy, RN

Author, Speaker, and founder of Mother Martha Family Foundation.

Chapter 1:

Overcoming Hardships:
The catalysts that changed my life.

This is a story about survival and triumph. The strength of the human will. But most of all, it's a love story—but not your typical love story. How a connection with a stranger from a faraway place helped to save my life. Love unifies people regardless of race, culture, economic status…it's the common thread that binds us all.

Be open-minded, skeptic. Be willing to listen to other people's opinions without taking them in as your own truth. This is just one of the many things I learned on my journey that began in 2003.

Andy Warhol stated that everyone will have fifteen minutes of fame. May 30, 2003 was my fifteen minutes of fame, in a sense. I was struck from behind while driving home from work.

The sound of squealing brakes before sudden darkness. Once I came to, I looked out of my driver side window to see the face of a firefighter. I had been struck from behind while driving in the second lane of a four-lane highway. My car was forced across two lanes then struck the concrete barrier in the middle. I was going in and out of consciousness. The firefighter's face was fading in and out. I heard the words, "We need three body bags over here," barked out by someone. Those are the only memories I have of the accident scene.

I was a young woman driving home from work on a Friday. I was excited about having the weekend off work. The sun was shining, and it was a beautiful afternoon. I was working in the daytime at a bank and in the evening, I was attending nursing school. That was my dream, to be a nurse. I was newly married, and we had just built our dream home. My life seemed to be on track, my future was bright. Within seconds my life changed. I went from being a healthy young woman with a bright future to lying in a hospital bed unable to move. My only view of the world was the ceiling in my hospital room.

When I regained consciousness, I saw a firefighter's face looking inside my driver's side window. His face was coming on and off like someone was turning a camera on and off. I could hear people talking in the background as I came to. My next memory was me being taken out of my car and into an ambulance. Flashes of voices, people's faces coming in and out. I remember a man's voice clearly, "We need three body bags over here."

I was pulled out of the ambulance in the triage area at the level one trauma center less than a mile away. My husband at that time was standing in the trauma bay waiting for my arrival to the hospital.

He had been working there for several years so I knew where I was when I saw his face. As they wheeled me in the trauma area, one of the paramedics was trying to comfort me. She said, "Darlin', we think you just have minor injuries but because of the nature of the accident you were involved in you're going to be surrounded by lots of doctors and nurses just to check you out." Because I had little memory of what happened, I was very grateful for her compassion.

One thing that television hospital dramas have in common with real life traumas is the drama. The commotion around you overloads your senses. You have people coming at you from all directions asking you questions. Loud noises, medical equipment coming at you, and bright lights shined in your eyes. I jumped as one doctor put a needle in my femoral artery. He asked me where the pain was. I said, "Where you are putting that needle, sir?" I am not sure how long all of this went on, but it emptied as quickly as it filled up. Leaving just two nurses behind.

One of them pushed me to a CT scanner. He stated similar words as the paramedic, "We believe you have minor injuries, but we want to make sure." I will always be grateful for the medical team that treated me that day. At that time, I would have never thought that several years later I would be one of those people asking trauma patients the exact same questions. Saving lives just like those angels who were around my bed that day.

I was then admitted to the trauma unit. A good assessment of my injuries had been done. My knees hurt the most. My head throbbed like my heart was pounding from inside it.

I could feel my physical injuries but I could not remember how I got them. As I lay in my hospital bed looking at the ceiling, memory flashes of what had transpired earlier that evening came to my mind. I could hear the usual sounds associated with a hospital, wheels turning on the equipment being pushed down the hallway, nurses and doctors talking at the nurses' station, and nurse call lights. The sound of brakes squealing kept replaying in my mind. The pain in my body was unbearable. Because I had a head injury, I was not allowed pain medications. They mask the symptoms of increased pressure in the brain, so resting was not an option.

I heard sounds of footsteps coming toward me then in my field of vision came a police officer. He stated, "Madam, my name is officer

Jenkins I am here to get a statement from you about what happened this evening." In West Virginia, people talk slow, deliberate, and with a southern accent.

I stated, "I don't remember much, and I cannot give you a written statement."

Officer Jenkins acknowledged my then husband sitting in the visitor's chair in the corner of the room, reached over to shake his hand. Then he pulled out a tape recorder from his bag. "When I push record, please tell me what you remember then identify yourself at the end."

"Officer, I do not remember much," I said as tears began to run down my face. "I was working at the bank, my boss told me that I had to stay a little longer to finish a project that was approaching deadline. I clocked out and was driving home as usual."

Officer Jenkins said, "Do you remember anything else?"

"I remember I was driving in the far-right hand lane of I-79, coming off the bridge where highway 79 splits off, you can turn left to go north or right to go south. Then just after the bridge, my world went dark, and I heard squealing brakes. Then I was coming in and out of consciousness in my car as a firefighter was trying to get my door open." The tears then became more intense. "Then the next thing I remember is being here at the hospital."

Officer Jenkins then thanked me for my statement and turned off the recorder. He put away his belongings, then turned to me. "Mrs. Hoy, you were one of the lucky ones in this accident. Three people did not make it."

My mind flashed back to hearing the person say, "We need three body bags over here," when the firefighter was trying to get me out of my car.

Tears ran down my cheeks, but I could not wipe them away. I stared at the ceiling on purpose to try to compose myself. I thought looking at the officer would make me lose my composure even more.

The officer told me that I was struck from behind at a high speed. Which explained my knee injuries—they must have been caused by being jammed underneath the dashboard from the rear impact. The front of my car had struck a concrete barrier. The air bags did not deploy so the left side of my head and my face hit the driver's side door. There was a large knot on the left side of my head that left me with a throbbing headache. I also had a neck injury from the rear impact.

Tim, my then husband, walked forward to my bedside to comfort me. He was not a compassionate man but was trying at that moment. We were newly married, and he was a darkhaired, handsome man. Short, yet a bit overconfident—part of what attracted me to him. He was a true country boy—flannel shirts, jeans, and a baseball cap were his usual attire. I told him I would be fine if he went home to get some rest. From then on, I was just waiting to hear what the trauma doctor's plan was for me. Tim reached down and kissed me on the forehead, said he would bring me a bag of personal care things the next day. After he left my hospital room, I pushed the nurse call bell to ask if someone could assist me to the restroom.

A slender young lady came to my bedside. I asked her to assist me to the bathroom. She advised against me getting up out of bed this soon after the car accident. Stubbornly, I insisted. She reluctantly helped me get out of bed. As we were passing by the mirror above the sink in the restroom, I caught a glimpse of my reflection. I stopped when I saw my reflection. My hair was full of blood and my face was unrecognizable. I began to touch my face as I looked in the mirror. I had no idea who the person was looking back at me. Most of the damage was on the left side of my face.

The nurse must have realized my reaction. she said "Come on now, let's keep going." As if to say hurry up, let's not look in the mirror right now.

Not only had my ability to move been restricted but I could not recognize myself when I looked in the mirror. I had lost my identity. I do not want to admit this because I am not found of cliches. But what happened was that I lost myself, and then I ended up finding myself.

My recovery had begun—physical therapy started to work with me so that I could be strong enough to go home. Because of the impact from behind, my knees were smashed under the dashboard, so walking was painful and difficult, but I was doing it. When walking was easier and less painful, I could sit a chair at the bedside to eat. I could see the faces of my nurses, the Jell-O on my plate and the view outside my window. When your life is reduced to only seeing a white tile ceiling you appreciate it much more when you can see the world around you. Something I told myself I would never take for granted again.

I recovered enough in a few days to go home. I was told by the trauma doctors that I needed multiple surgeries that included surgery on both knees and my face. The road to recovery was going to be long. I was determined to get better and finish nursing school. After my life was saved by all those wonderful nurses and doctors at the hospital, I was determined to finish what I had started. The positive side of stubbornness is when it is expressed as persistence.

The front page of the local newspaper the next day after the car accident.

The root of the word recovery we use today stems from the 1520s, meaning "act of righting oneself after a blunder, or mishap." Glancing back, I am not sure if I would call it "righting myself," but it was a turning point in my life.

I was released from the hospital once medical staff knew it was safe due to the head injury. I still had a throbbing headache and was wearing a C collar to stabilize my neck, but I could safely move around without assistance. The support from well-wishers started to pour in once I was settled in at home. I remember thinking, I didn't know I was so loved.

Events such as these reveal a lot about you and those around you. Those who love and support you do so, while those who do not walk away. Some even try to kick you when you're down.

A friend and mentor came to visit me and gave me a book, Man's Search for Meaning by Viktor Frankl.

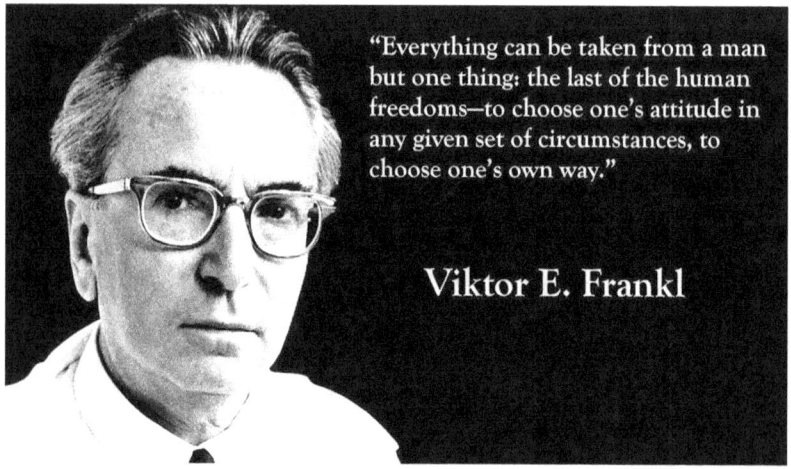

The book is from 1946, in which Dr. Frankl describes his experiences within Auschwitz concentration camp during World War II. Not the upbeat cheery material you would expect to receive from a friend while recovering from injuries. Because she was such a great inspiration in my life, I gave the book a chance.

I was home waiting recovering—I had time to read. I could not put the book down. It was a mixture of world history and a story of personal perseverance all in one—an observation of human psychology during the worst of circumstances any human could imagine living in.

Dr. Frankl noticed that people who survived the concentration camp saw meaning in their circumstances. They talked about their future with hope that they would see their families again, visualizing what will happen in the future. He observed that people who lost hope smoked their last cigarette then died shortly after. Everything had been taken from these people: their belongings, their families, access to food, basic life necessities, even their names. But they had the one thing that no one can take from them—their right to choose their own attitude in their given circumstances.

I learned that I could choose how I responded. If Dr. Frankl could live through what I could only imagine as hell on earth and had then gone on to help a lot of people and accomplish great things, then I could do the same.

I spent the summer of 2003 at home waiting to find out if the trauma physicians would allow me to go to nursing school that fall. Due to physical therapy and my determination to get better, I was walking without assistive devices at the beginning of August. I had started out using a walker, then crutches and lastly, a cane. My gait did not look normal when I walked but I was strong enough to drive myself to physical therapy and perform daily activities for myself.

After much consideration from my physicians, they decided to allow me to attend nursing school that fall at the University of Charleston. I had been taking classes at night after my banking job at the local college to get the general studies courses finished. I was determined to carry out the goals I had started before the accident, on May 30, 2003. The downside of going back to school that semester was that I had to put off surgeries until Christmas break. That meant two surgeries a week apart and having to return to my studies a week later. I was determined to see my goal through so that fall I began to attend nursing school.

Chapter 2:

The Recovery.

"Those that have a 'why' can bear almost any 'how.'"
-Viktor E. Frankl

As far as men in my life up to this point none of them would be considered gentlemen.

My father was not the type of man who would be given one of those trophies that states "World's Best Father" on it. He was raised in the local orphanage. My biological grandmother had given birth to many children but only chose to raise two of them. My father was the eldest of the ten children of my paternal grandmother. She gave him up to the state when he was seven years old. His earliest memories of his life are caring for other children in the household while his mother was out with "gentlemen callers".

My father drank every day. Each evening we knew when he had come home from his job at the factory because we could hear the refrigerator door open. The sound of a beer bottle cap being turned. From that moment on no one in the household knew what to expect and we walked on eggshells until bedtime. Since he saw women as "the bad guys" because of what his mother did to him, my mother and I were frequently his targets. I spent a lot of my childhood standing up and protecting my mother from his rants. Most of it was emotional and mental abuse, but at times it did turn physical. The problem with emotional and mental abuse is that is causes more damage to a person, but it is not easily proven to others around you. Looking back now, I wish I had not stood in front of my mother so much because she never had that strength to stand up to him on her own.

Most of the time his behavior while drinking involved insulting me and my mother. No task was ever up to his standard. We could spend hours cleaning and cooking, yet the house was never clean enough and his meals were never fit for him. I remember me and my mother spending all day at the salon to come home to him saying to us, "Why do you even go to the salon? You always come home looking the same."

Miller Lite beer in a can and Winston cigarettes were what my father smelled like most of the time. He was short, around five feet six inches tall, and always wore his dark straight hair combed backward. Physically, he was not someone who could overpower us easily. But by the time I had reached my teenage years there was some physical abuse. I remember attending high school with two black eyes for a week. Once he pushed me hard and my back had a bruise the shape of the doorknob at the bottom. Another student in my gym class told the school counselor what she had seen. I was called into the counselor's office the next day. I explained the injury and she sent me back to my classroom.

One Friday night my father and my uncle were outside drinking whiskey. In our front yard we had a concrete support wall next to a sidewalk that led to the front door. They were both sitting on it calmly having a drink together when I looked out the kitchen window. An hour later we heard a loud scream come from outside followed by the sound of scattering glass. This caused my mother and me to run outside to see what had happened.

My father was lying on the sidewalk face-up surrounded by blood. Most of the blood seemed to be coming from his head. Scattered glass surrounded his body that was obviously the bottle of Jack Daniels whiskey I had seen them drinking from an hour earlier.

I called the emergency number to get my father the medical treatment he needed. He recovered from that incident within a couple of weeks. He then began to seek treatment for his problem with alcohol. I turned eighteen years old a few months after this incident. I decided to move out and start my adult life.

I got married in my early twenties. My husband was a hardworking man a few years older than me. He came from a tight-knit family that lived in a small town not far away. He asked me to marry him from the driver's seat of his white two-door Cougar. I said yes right away, and then we went to his mother to tell her about the upcoming marriage. She said, "You'll have to get along better than you do now if this is going to happen." She was a brute of a woman who never had a good thing to say about anyone.

After we married, we bought a piece of land a couple of hours away from our families. We decided to build a house by ourselves, which we accomplished in five years. Every inch of that house was put together by our own hands. We worked on it in the evenings after his shift at the medical center and I worked on it between my bank job and night school. We were both goal-oriented and worked well together.

He was a good man in a lot of ways. I never went without my material needs met. But the marriage lacked compassion. Just like my father, nothing I did was ever good enough. He would frequently come home to inspect my housework. If the dishwasher was not loaded or the closets were not organized to his satisfaction, he would raise his voice and begin cursing and insulting me. I baked him a cake from a recipe of his mother's, yet it was still not up to his standards. After that he frequently told everyone, including his family, how worthless in the kitchen I was. Just like my father my material needs were met but neither man showed me any compassion.

With little personal support, coupled with the injuries I received from the car accident, I knew nursing school would be more challenging for me. But anything worth having is not easily obtained. I finished the fall semester an honor student.

Not recognizing myself in the mirror was a defining moment for me. Ultimately, not recognizing my physical self, led me to look within to find my own strength. The only plastic surgeon I trusted to do surgery on my face was Dr. Hans Lee, who was known to be one of the best in the area. That's why I agreed to the only available time he had, Christmas Eve.

My then husband took me to the hospital to have surgery that morning. It was becoming difficult for me to breathe, especially at night. During those three hours in the operating room, my nose and face were reconstructed. I woke up in the recovery room unable to see clearly and it felt like my heart was about to jump out of my chest. I looked over at the nurse next to me to try to communicate with her how much pain was in my chest.

She immediately told me that some blood vessels in my nose started to bleed so much it was becoming critical. In order to stop the bleeding, the doctor had to use cocaine to constrict the vessels. I remember thinking, You put cocaine in my nose? Cocaine is a stimulant coupled with blood loss, so that is why my heart was beating fast enough to cause chest pain.

I was sent home with my face bandaged to the point that only my eyes could be seen. When I returned to Dr. Lee's office a few days later to have the bandages removed it felt like an unveiling. As he removed the bandages, underneath was revealed an image in the mirror that I finally recognized. It's a moment I will never forget.

It was not from a place of vanity, but it felt as though Dr Lee had given me back my identity. As I looked in the mirror, tears began to stream down my face. I could see myself clearly for the first time.

I had always had poor self-esteem. When you are repeatedly told you are ugly, stupid, and worthless you begin to believe it. During those months when I did not recognize myself in the mirror, I spent a good deal of my time alone. I learned a lot about myself. In a sense I had to lose myself in order to find myself. Not being able to recognize my face led me to go within and what I learned was that I was none of the things others around me had told me I was.

The pain in my left knee was constant and it never improved with physical therapy or pain medications. New Year's Eve 2004, just a week after facial surgery, I had surgery on my left knee. The probability of success was fifty percent based on the severity of the injury. Due to the severity of the pain, I was willing to take the chance.

Surgery was performed without complications, and I woke up in the recovery room a couple of hours later with a brace on my left leg that started at my upper thigh and ended at my ankle. The most painful part came next. As soon as you are settled into your hospital bed, physical therapy starts. The sooner you're moving the better the range of motion in your leg, with faster recovery, and less pain. I apologized to the physical therapist that came to take that brace off my leg. She began to bend it and I screamed. I apologized to her because I felt like I was just being a wimp. She assured me that I was not being a wimp and that pain now meant better results later.

Thankfully, after a month of physical therapy, the surgery was a success. The pain had improved, my gait had improved, and I had greater range of motion in my left leg.

I returned to nursing school that spring. People noticed right away when they saw me that my face had changed and that I was walking better. My then husband was there at my side for every surgery, caring for me by doing things such as ensuring I received my mediations on time. But nothing had changed in our home life or within our marriage.

One evening, I withdrew money from an ATM on campus to buy food for a study session with friends. When I returned home that evening, he went into a rage about the three-dollar ATM withdrawal fee that went on for around thirty minutes. Nothing I did or said seemed to be good enough for him. Just like when I lived with my father, I walked on eggshells around my husband, never knowing when he would erupt into a fiery rant of emotional abuse.

The abuse began to affect my self-esteem. I started to ask myself *What is wrong with me? If everyone is telling me I am worthless, and good at nothing, then what do I need to change to be enough?*

During spring break of 2004, I had surgery on my right knee. The injury to my right knee was not as severe as the left one so the surgery was shorter and required less recovery time. The surgery was performed without complications but after a month of physical therapy there was no improvement. The right knee surgery was not considered a success, but despite that, I returned to nursing school in the fall of 2004.

My why was to overcome the injuries sustained in the car accident in order to become a nurse. Two years after the car accident, I graduated from the University of Charleston with an associate degree in nursing. I remember how proud I was walking across that stage at my graduation. I had graduated with honors, which is not an easy thing to do, especially when I had undergone three surgeries. "You cannot climb a smooth mountain" was the quote I remembered as I stepped out on that stage to receive my degree. Not long after that, I started working at the medical center where I had been a trauma patient.

Chapter 3:

My life as a nurse with a lot of replacement parts.

"What you have experienced, no power on earth can take from you."
-Viktor E. Frankl

Once you know what its like to go through something then it is easier to put yourself in that person's shoes. My experience being a patient the previous two years had made me a more compassionate nurse. It was an honor to be working side by side with those that had saved my life. Now I was one of the life savers.

It was not easy to do such a physically demanding job after everything my body had went through. Often my knees would swell, and hips would ache. But when I would pass through the trauma ward where I had been a patient, I remembered that not long before I was a patient in one of those beds. My only view of the world was the ceiling. I was now grateful that I was now able to be the nurse.

My home life was more of the same, walking on eggshells. 'Such is life' I would think in my head as I got in the morning to the sound of Sports center playing in the living room. Tim, my then husband always got up before me. I was never a morning person.

But because I never knew what would trigger one of his verbal abusive rants, I did not look forward to coming out of my bedroom to face my day.

Looking back, it is easy to say, "Why didn't you leave?" or to ask, "Couldn't you see the signs?" I guess it was a mixture of things. The signs were there but sometimes you can't see the forest for the trees. I made excuses for his verbal abusive rants. He has a stressful job, or he just had a bad day.

I wanted to make it work, I had made a commitment. I thought, "He will some day see how kind, and loving I am, and things will get better." All the while my self esteem was falling further down.

I reached out to family and friends many times to tell them what was going on in my life. Many did not believe me. My parents would say, "Just stick it out. You married him." From the outside looking in our lives looked ideal. We had built a beautiful home, we both graduated from college and had good jobs. It looked like we had the American dream. From the outside it looked picture perfect. But sometimes it is only the picture that is perfect. That American dream from the inside was a nightmare.

I was trying to stay on my feet working as a nurse with all the things my body had been through. This relationship had me beat down to the point that I felt like I was a shell of a human. Just going through life just existing. I did not know who I was, what I liked or did not like. I was told who I was, and what I liked. With my self-esteem at its lowest I was still waiting for things to get better.

This book is not about what he did or placing blame. I have never claimed to be an angel who did nothing wrong. This book is about what I learned from my experiences.

Chapter 4:

Life without connection brings loneliness.

> "Despair is suffering without meaning."
> -Viktor E. Frankl

Loneliness is rooted in thinking no one cares. It makes no difference if a person is sitting next to you or on the other side of world when it comes to loneliness.

A person sitting next to you can still be a stranger. And once you form a true connection with someone, where they are located on the planet makes little difference. It's best when the person you have a connection with is beside you. But when the person beside you just exists, that's when loneliness takes root.

Just a few years into my nursing career, I began to have health issues. I was unable to work. I felt trapped in my body and trapped in my home. Literally and figuratively it felt as though I had built my own prison. At that point the medical community was telling me, "You will never be a nurse again." The evidence they had to prove it was impressive.

There was little emotional support from those around me. Frequently I was put down with statements such as, "But you don't look sick." "You're not sick; you're just lazy." And my favorite: "Don't they have a pill for that?"

During the next four years, I spent most of my time in my bedroom alone. Knowing that I must control my thoughts before my mind fell into a deep depression, I began to read any book I could get my hands on. Study any subject I could get information about. Keeping my mind active while a prisoner in my body and home.

My then husband supported me financially. He would wake me up in the mornings before he went to work to give me my medication. Emotionally, there was no support from anyone. When I would cry from physical pain my then husband would get angry at me and state, "What's wrong with you now?"

With each day I was able to do more than the following day. I started out with small goals, such as walking to the mailbox every day, and the goal for the next day, I would add a little more distance.

Chapter 5:

A connection was found in an unexpected place.

> "Love is the only way to grasp another human being in the innermost core of his personality."
> -Viktor E. Frankl

I was surrounded by books filled with lessons from others. I had the greatest mentors in the world around me. I concluded that true healing must come from within. Allow love from the heart to lead you. Love unites people. I had plenty of evidence around me that lack of compassion separated people.

Lack of compassion is a cycle that is destructive and continues until it's broken. The men in my life were proof of that; they never healed the hole inside themselves that was planted from lack of compassion. Especially by the women by who society's standards were supposed to love them: their mothers.

From my isolation social media began opening the world to me, connecting me to people and places that I would have never gotten to know before and were now just a click away. Information flowed in from all areas of the world. Events that happened on the other side of the planet only took a few seconds to appear on my cell phone screen. It was amazing to see but at times it felt like so much information appearing that I was drowning in information yet starving for wisdom.

I became friends with a young man named Geofrey Mugisha. Your first thought might be that with was some 90-day Finance type of thing. That his guy was just asking for money. That was not the case. I knew when I spoke to this young man had the heart and mind of a leader.

I found out he was an orphan in Uganda living in orphanage called Bulamu Children's village. That a family in Minnesota was in the process of adopting his brother.

We began to talk every day. It was the beginning of a friendship. We talked about our love of animals and compared our cultures. When you take the time to just sit and talk to a person you find out how similar we all are. Pointing out our differences creates separation, which leads to a lack of compassion. Through our small differences we began to learn from one another.

When someone comes into the emergency room for treatment everyone is treated the same. The homeless, the drug addicts, prostitutes, lawyers. Whatever label you want to give others we are all the same. No one goes, "Well this guy's heart is different because of his job or lack of one, or his skin color or the amount of money in his wallet." It's all the same.

During our conversations, he told me what life was like in Bulamu Children's Village and in Uganda. He and his brother were both living there. But his brother was patiently waiting to go live with his adoptive family in Minnesota. I did verify the information he was telling me. His brother was adopted by that family a year later. But I never pushed him to talk about it. Growing up with a father that was also an orphan, I understood how that affected a person.

A man named Joseph Lubega took Geofrey and his brother off the street and to Bulamu Children's Village. Everyone who knows him calls him Uncle Joseph, a man who does everything with loving intent. A true man of God who has dedicated his life to caring for children—a big task since Uganda has 2.5 million orphans.

We continued to build our friendship, and never did he ask for anything other a listening ear. We began to exchange ideas. I had a double closet filled from the floor to the ceiling of writings plus an entire room filled with books. All knowledge that I began to share with him. I learned he too had a passion for learning. He taught himself English by picking up pieces of paper others had littered on the street. His English was more proper than mine, the Queen's English. It lacked any slang words. Being from the southeastern part of the United States, I have a thick accent that is noticeable right away. We talked about subjects such as science, philosophy, psychology, history, politics, and law. I have a passion for science, and he had a passion for law and politics. I looked forward to our daily conversations no matter how brief.

Geofrey lacked a mother figure in his life. I had a lack of connection. Together we found a friendship in each other. Neither of us expected to find friendship or a connection in each other. From the outside looking in we were different people. Different cultures, countries, race, and age difference. I became the mother figure he needed, and he became the trusted friend that I lacked in my life.

I continued with physical therapy and everyday doing a little more than I had done before. I guess you could say that it was the fact that I then had someone who cared in my life. That I had found new meaning in it all, I received medical clearance to return to work.

Since Geofrey had been such a good friend to me, I decided that such a brilliant mind should have the opportunity of an education. It was laid upon my heart to help Geofrey to study law in a formal setting. I never questioned my decision. I told him that the only thing I asked for in return was to pay it forward in some way. Do a kind deed for another, no matter how big or small.

When I asked Geofrey to "pay it forward" I thought maybe he would buy someone a meal or do some king act for another. What he did shocked me. In November 2017, Geofrey and his brother started AMKA Foundation Africa. They gathered donations to take to refugees from South Sudan who were coming into Northern Uganda. Bidi Bidi was then the largest refugee settlement camp in the world, with 270,000 South Sudanese refugees fleeing civil war in their country.

Photos from AMKA Foundation's visit to Bidi Bidi. On December 21, 2017 they rented a van and filled it with what little supplies they had gathered through donations. An act of kindness to the refugees at Christmas time.

Geofrey on television in Uganda speaking about his trip to Bidi, Bidi.

Children at Bidi, Bidi.

Picture of women supporting each other at Bidi, Bidi.

A few days before Christmas I was at home in West Virginia. Just sat down on my couch to take a break from decorating for the holidays when I received these pictures from Geofrey. I could not believe that something I did could end up helping so many people. I asked Geofrey to pay it forward, just one kind act. He had exceeded my expectations. I began to sob tears of joy.

After I composed myself, I was still in a state of shock. I just kept thinking "how could someone like me do something like this?" I thought little of myself because those around me told me just how much of a low life I was and often.

Soon after AMKA's trip to Bidi Bidi, Geofrey graduated from college. In my mind, he had paid it forward. I was proud of him just as if he was my son. He had called me "Mother Teresa" in the past because I had been there to help him. I told him I was no saint and that I was not comfortable with being called Mother Teresa. Mother Martha is what he decided to call me. That was the type of relationship he and I had, Mother and son.

Chapter 6:

I had a realization that changed everything.

> "Between Stimulus and response there is a space. In that space is our power to choose our response. In our response lies growth and our freedom."
> -Viktor Frankl

During the time Geofrey was taking donations to the refugees at Bidi Bidi, I was on a trip to Washington, DC. I desperately needed a break and Christmas time in Washington, DC is beautiful. Outside Christmas concerts, families gathered for caroling with hot chocolate. Tim, my then husband decided to go on the trip with me. He did not like to travel so he rarely traveled with me. I felt a little uneasy about it since the marriage and our home life had become rocky. But I was looking forward to enjoying all that Capitol Hill has to offer at Christmas.

I visited my friend Martin Weiss—a holocaust survivor who tells his story once a week at the National Holocaust Museum. When he was freed from Auschwitz, he showed compassion toward others by sharing his food after he had been starved by the Nazis. He educates others, brings people together, and helps others to heal. It is with great honor that I can call him my friend.

I was inspired to create this watercolor for Martin.

Only through unity do we have diversity and abundance. Each person a beautiful unique hue (hu-man) in the landscape of creation.

Martha Hoy
2018

It was turning out it be a nice trip. I got to see my friend, attend an outdoor Christmas concert, and toured all the historical sites of the United States Capital. That evening is when things took a turn.

We were walking around the reflecting pool on Capitol Hill. It was a beautiful winter evening, lightly snowing. It was quiet because no one was around except for a few secret service agents. I went to reach for my husband's hand, so we could enjoy the moment together. He rejected my hand and stated, "It's too cold," then walked back to our hotel by himself leaving me standing alone.

There was more to it than that, but this book is not about what he did. Human beings like to make people famous for doing the wrong things. I am telling you this part because at that moment is when I realized just how bad everything had gotten. If he was willing to make a scene on Capital Hill with armed Secret Service agents within sight, then I knew it was time to leave.

Sometimes it feels like we get deep into something that we can't see what is really going on. It was like at that moment something snapped in my mind. With tears in my eyes, I said out loud, "he doesn't even like me." I began walking slowly back to my hotel room. Which was awkward because I knew he would be waiting in the hotel room.

The rest of the trip was awkward silence. Once we landed in back home in West Virginia, I knew what I had to do. It was time to plan to get out of there.

For years I had told everyone around me that my home life was bad. No one believed me. Most people thought I was making things a bigger deal then they were. Because of that I really had no where to go. It is not like I could just go to a friend or a family member's house.

I began to put together documents of the things necessary to make a break. A list of things we owned, important papers that would be needed. I packed a little white suitcase full of essential items and placed it in my closet at the foot of my bed. I tried to do slowly and to go unnoticed.

I would avoid him as much as possible. I could hear him cursing me in the shower from the living room in the evenings. He began to focus his anger on my dog Sophie. One morning as I lie in bed, I heard him curse and hit her. Of course, I got out of bed to intervene. I wasn't sure if he knew I was planning to leave that's why his rants of anger were getting more frequent, but it was evidence that things were beginning to escalate.

Chapter 7:

She's on the run.

It was Mother's Day, which is ironic since Geofrey calls me "Mother Martha" just like the day of the car accident, my life was changed in an instant. Sometimes I think God or the Universe, whatever label you feel comfortable with, has too much faith in my strength. But I had been trying to plug the hole in the bottom of that sinking ship for too long. That relationship was bound to go suddenly crashing into the icy waters. On that day, it certainly did.

I was lying in my bed watching television wearing my pajamas, with my dog Chloe at my side. Then suddenly my then husband Tim entered the room. I knew from the way he approached me that if I did not run at that moment, I would not survive the interaction.

There was a struggle and I lounged forward in order reach for the suitcase in my closet. There was a struggle down the hallway as I tried to force myself to the front door.

He was screaming at me, "You will never amount to anything, no one else will ever put up with you!"

Words I was used to hearing daily.

The struggle continued into the living room. I finally got enough strength to push my way to the front door. While fighting him off I rolled that suitcase to the end of the porch and then stopped.

I looked him right in the eyes and said, "You will never see my face again."

Shaking and crying, I hurried up and placed that suitcase in the back seat of car. Got in the driver's seat, floored the gas pedal, with tires squealing as I pulled out of the driveway.

I drove a few miles away to a safe distance and pulled over. I slumped over my steering wheel and began to cry. I had no idea where I was going to go from there. I had just left my entire life behind but going back was not an option.

My first thought was, "Who is the one person that I could always trust?" The answer was Geofrey. But he was 7,000 miles away in Uganda. I had no idea what he could do to help me. But I called him.

He immediately said, "Go to Minnesota to my brother's apartment. He will keep you safe."

The second phone call was to Ivan in Minnesota. I told him what had happened just an hour earlier. He agreed to allow me to come stay with him, no questions asked.

Ivan said, "Because of everything you have done for my brother you can come here." I hung up the phone with Ivan, stopped to get gas, and then began to try to figure out how I was going to get to Minnesota. After I was done pumping gas into my car, I called my friend Barb.

Barb and I had been friends since high school. She still lived in our hometown of Fairmont, West Virginia. Fairmont was just a two-hour drive from where I had been living in Charleston for the past decade. She was a single mother of one daughter. Her daughter had gone off to college the previous fall. Barb was in a career transition. Fairmont is a small town, the only things it's known for are pepperoni rolls and being the hometown of Mary Lou Retton, a gymnast that won a gold medal in the 1984 Summer Olympics. At that time, she was packing to move to Las Vegas, Nevada—quite a change from our small hometown.

I arrived at Barb's front door around nine o'clock that evening, still in my pajamas. My eyes were red and swollen from crying and my hair was a mess. Barb answered the door looking about the same, disheveled hair, wearing sweatpants and a big T-shirt. Around thirty-five years old, blonde, medium-length hair, and a round face. We were always opposite in our appearance. In high school I was thin, with long brown hair and a long face. We both looked a bit different now some years later, but I like to think we had both aged well.

Barb opened the door, "Well, get in here. Are you hungry?"

"No," I said walked my suitcase to her daughter's room. Her daughter had gone away to college the fall of the previous year, so it was mine for a few days. We both sat down in her living room after I put my things away.

"Tell me what happened. You look like hell."

Barb was never one to hold anything back. She was a straight shooter who cursed like a sailor, but she has a good heart.

As I recounted what had happened just a few hours before I did not cry. I think I had run out of tears at that point.

"What are your plans now?" Barb said with a look of concern her face. "I am going to Minnesota to stay with Ivan, Geofrey's brother." That statement turned her look of concern to one of shock. "Well, alright then. You can stay here for three days and help me pack up my things for my move to Las Vegas. I'm going to bed now. Help yourself to whatever is in the kitchen." She went into her bedroom and closed the door.

That left me there on the couch alone to process what had just transpired that last eight hours of my life. As I relived what had just happened, I realized I had just left everything I had ever known, my entire life reduced to a suitcase. Staying safe was the most important thing at that moment. I knew I had to put a large distance between me and the past. I booked my flight to Minneapolis/Saint Paul Airport for three days from then from my phone as I sat there on the couch. I thought to myself, It's time to put a whole lot of miles and a whole lot of Jesus between me and this place.

We spent three days doing the things we did as teenagers, such as talking about boys, eating pizza, and drinking coca-colas. I helped her pack her belongings for her move across the country.

As I was pulling a lot of sweatpants and sweatshirts out of her closet, I stated, "Barb, you need to update your wardrobe. You are moving to Las Vegas, darlin'."

Barb looked at me with a scowl on her face. "I have been a single mother for ten years, Martha, leave me alone."

"Barb, well now your daughter is in college and you will be living in Las Vegas, time for a redo of this closet. We will have to have a funeral for your lady parts if you don't."

We both laughed at my ridiculous joke. Barb took a piece of pizza out of the box, "Fine, I will get rid of a couple pairs of these sweatpants."

I grabbed a pair of sweatpants with holes in them, threw them at her. "Here, start with these."

After a few days in my hometown pretending to be teenagers again, I set off for Chuck Yeager Airport just two miles south back in the town I had just run from—Charleston, West Virginia.

I got ready that morning and Barb walked me to the front door.

"Call me when you get to Ivan's place." Barb said to me in a motherly tone.

"I will call you as soon I get settled."

We hugged each other in the doorway, not knowing when we would see each other again.

I made a stop along the way at my attorney's office to file for divorce.

I sat at the end of a long wooden table waiting for my attorney to come in with the papers I needed to sign. She walked in the room with a stack of paperwork and laid it on the table in front of me.

Then looked at me and stated, "You cannot leave the state of West Virginia with your car, it is marital property, the judge will not allow it." I replied, "Fine, but before I allow him to hurt me, I will put a brick on the gas pedal and push that car into the Kanawha River." I then pointed out of the window of her office to the view of Kanawha River. The fact that a car is more important than a person's life should make everyone think carefully before marrying anyone.

I signed the necessary papers to file for divorce, then I drove that car to the parking garage of the airport. I texted my attorney the number of the parking spot it was parked in and told her I would FedEx the keys when I landed at my destination. I was boarding a plane to my freedom. Cars can be replaced—people cannot be replaced.

Minneapolis-Saint Paul International Airport was my destination. Some place I had never even visited, to live with people I had never met. Some might say that was courageous. I guess looking back, I believe it was. But it was necessary. I left behind everything I had and ever knew. Turning back was not an option.

As the plane was ascending out of West Virginia it felt like pure freedom. Like I was ascending out of hell. That flight was the beginning of my new life.

Chapter 8:

Healing in Minnesota begins and a new family emerges.

"What is to give light must endure burning."
-Viktor E. Frankl

I found a place to sit at the Minneapolis/Saint Paul Airport, near a black grand piano. I was anxious because I was waiting for a young man to pick me up who I had never met. All I had was a picture of him on my phone, a stranger who I was going to live with and trust that he was going to protect me. I was in a place that I had never been. Although I was scared, I knew it a better option than going back to what I had just left behind.

I went into the bathroom to freshen up before letting him know I had landed. I needed to freshen up before I told Ivan that I had landed. My appearance was disheveled, my light brown hair piled in knots on my head, and my eyes were so swollen I could barely see that they were blue. I felt free from the chains of the past, leaving it in West Virginia. I was exhausted and I felt empty inside. My appearance reflected that.

I texted him that I am sitting next to the black grand piano. Along with a picture of the piano. There I sat on the bench looking around for the face that matched the one on my phone.

A tall, slender African young man with big, beautiful eyes and a killer smile came around the corner a few minutes later. That smile looked just like Geofrey's smile. I knew instantly that it was Ivan. A sense of relief filled my body at that at the sight of his smiling face.

We hugged each other. He said, "I cannot believe you are here." We walked in silence to his car.

As he loaded up my suitcase in his car. He said, "I wish I had a better car to pick you up in."

I stated, "Darlin', I am just grateful you are helping me. What's next?" I meant something like, What's for dinner? He thought I was contemplating life. He said, "Now we live."

Looking back now I guess that was a simple yet profound statement. It was time for me to live. Truly live my life.

I could heal and find out who I was without all the noise from those who had been around me previously. Sometimes in life we just exist. I had done plenty of that. Now it was time to live.

It reminded me of something my mentor used to say: "Life is a like a bad camping trip. It is a temporary trip. Bad things happen—bugs bite you, you do not catch your dinner, there are bears in the woods that scare us, your tent may fall, but why can't we enjoy all the good things as well? The beautiful sunset, the flowers and the good company of those around us. Pain in life is inevitable, but misery is a choice." Her words of wisdom went through my head as I was seeing the town of Minneapolis for the first time.

I was nervous and excited about what was ahead. As I looked out the windows of Ivan's rusted old car taking in the sights and sounds.

We arrived at Ivan's third floor apartment in Blaine, Minnesota by late afternoon. As we opened the door, his roommate Joe was there to greet me. It was comforting to see another smiling face. He introduced himself and told me to make myself at home. Joe is the definition of tall, dark and handsome—broad shoulders, wide facial features, a muscular body, and a warm smile. I felt safe immediately as I walked through the front door.

Ivan directed me to his room and said that I could settle there. I unpacked my things while Ivan made up the couch for himself. We ate dinner together that evening. Conversation was the usual getting to know you stuff. What do you do for a living? Where did you grow up? That type of conversation. That night as I lay in the bed of a stranger, in a town I had never been in before, I felt of sense of calm. Calm because I was safe. That I never had to go back to that life in West Virginia again.

I ended up spending the next four months with Joe and Ivan in Blaine, Minnesota. It is not the most exciting place to live, there's not much there but a Walmart, an ice-skating rink, and a Dairy Queen. Blaine is not far from Minneapolis and Saint Paul, the twin cities. Not sure why they are called that, because the two cities seem completely different to me. Saint Paul is a town with its roots deep in the Catholic religion—old temples and beautiful Roman-style architecture. Minneapolis is more modern with tall buildings and skyscrapers. Although it was not the most exciting place to be, It was a great place to heal.

You never know how toxic a situation is until you are out of it. It was like I was breathing fresh air for the first time in a long time. Healing is messy and takes time. Looking back now I wish I would have been more patient with myself.

No one from my home or my family even tried to find me. I just walked away from my life and not one person bothered to try to find out what had happened to me. Not even my parents. No matter how good of a person you are, there are people who will never support you. Even those you think should support you, or those that society thinks should support you. It was hurtful. I kept thinking, How could a mother or father not care about what happens to their child? I went to my mother repeatedly to tell her what was going on. She said to stick it out.

In Minnesota I not only began to heal but I started to build a new family. Ivan and Joe had become like family to me. Getting used to single life again and living with two single young African men from two different cultures was a big change. But a welcomed change. We learned a lot about each other. Ivan cooked us food from Uganda. Joe and Ivan argued about whose country had the most gorillas, Uganda or Rwanda. All our conversations were educational.

I love food and I fell in love with the food from both cultures. We had conversations about the things they had seen and experienced since coming to live in the United States. It is educational to see your own culture from the perspective of those who are from other places in the world. I often found myself saying, "I am not sure why we do things that way?" I learned a lot about myself as well.

Joe is a very social guy—frequently going out with friends or having friends coming over to visit. Ivan is a quiet guy who would rather stay at home, watching movies and writing music. I used to say it would take a threat from the North Korean government to get him out of that apartment to go anywhere but work. Both young men were supportive and respectful. They frequently called me Momma Martha which made me giggle sometimes because I am not that much older than Joe. But I understood it came from a place of respect.

I learned a lot about Uganda through my conversations with Geofrey but living with Ivan taught me much more. I was sitting on the couch with Ivan one evening he was watching television. I was writing something, just glancing at the television briefly from time to time. I was writing but glancing up at the television periodically.

I looked up to see violence on the screen. It was a group of men beating up men and women in what looked like the inside of a government building. Suddenly I forgot about writing and began to watch what was happening on the television screen. It was so barbaric and violent I could not look away.

I looked over at Ivan and said, "This is the government in Uganda?" with a mixed look of disgust and surprise on my face.

Ivan looked over at me and stated, "Unfortunately, that is parliament in Uganda."

I knew little about the political history of the country. I knew they had been suppressed by a dictatorship for the past thirty-three years. I knew a few stories about Milton Obote, the former Prime Minister, and I knew about the bloody history of former President Idi Amin.

On the screen, I saw a man get hit in the head with a chair. I shouted out of shock, "OH MY! That poor man." That man was Zaake Francis Butebi, a member of parliament in Uganda. He and I would end up being friends shortly after I saw him being physically assaulted on television that day, in the summer of 2018.

Seeing that video of how brutal the government was on the floor of parliament was more insight to the state of the country.

Some people have told me they think the way I got a divorce was badass. On July 7, 2018, I clocked out for lunch at my job, went to my car, and called my attorney on her cell phone. I refused to return to the state of West Virginia because I still felt it was unsafe to return. My attorney had expressed feeling unsafe when my then husband would show up at her office, so getting permission from the judge to attend the divorce hearing over the phone was granted. I remember hearing the judge's pen gliding across the paper over the phone as he signed his name on the divorce papers.

I said, "Sir you have no idea how you changed the world by signing those papers." I am not sure why that came out of my mouth at that moment, it was just a feeling I had. Not sure if I would say it was the most badass thing that I did during my journey. It was the last thing needed for closure from my previous life.

After four months with Joe and Ivan, I decided it was time to move on with my life. I had healed enough to leave the safety of their apartment.

I was newly single, and my friend Barb had set up in Las Vegas. Two single ladies restarting their lives in "Sin City." The city full of excitement and bright lights.

Chapter 9:

Viva Las Vegas.

"Life is not primarly a quest for pleasure, as Freud believed, or a quest for power, as Alfred Adler taught, but a quest for meaning."
- Vicktor E. Frankl

Driving down Las Vegas Boulevard for the first time—seeing the bright lights and the crowds of people on the sidewalks, listening to the song Viva Las Vegas playing in my car— was so exiting.

My future was an open book with blank pages. A blank canvas in which I could paint whatever picture I wanted. With each word or brush stroke I could determine what my life was going to look like. I had been through so much trauma—abuse, my friends and family had rejected me, and my body would never be without the effects from the car accident. I had learned to adjust to my physical ailments. My life may have been reduced to just a suitcase full of personal effects, but I still had my life. Now I was free to make it look like whatever I wanted it to.

This was time to find out who I was. People had told who I was for years. Told me how I should think, feel, and what I should do. When you are in an abusive situation in your home, your every move is criticized and controlled. I allowed the perceptions of others define who I was.

Just four months earlier I was helping Barb pack in West Virginia now I was unpacking what little I had from that suitcase. I always wanted to live somewhere that people came to vacation, and I wanted a palm tree in the front yard. That dream was coming true.

Just four months earlier Barb and I had been packing up her apartment in West Virginia to move to Las Vegas. Now I was in Las Vegas unpacking the few belongings I had into her apartment.

The goal was to be two single ladies living close to the Las Vegas strip restarting out lives. We had been friends for a long time. I shared in the joy when Barb's daughter was born. Barb celebrated with me when I got married. Moving in together made sense. We were both at a point in our lives that it was sort of a redo and we had been friends most of our lives.

I got a job at a nearby hospital and settled into life in Las Vegas easily. I had spent my life up until then living in figurative chains. At that point, I thought I was more healed than I was. But my journey of self-discovery had began in the coolest city on Earth, Las Vegas.

Barb is more of an introvert and then me. She worked from home in her sweatpants most of her career. But I was ready to explore Las Vegas. I wanted to experience and see everything I could. After getting settled into my new home and my job that's what I did.

The porch of the Venetian Hotel became my favorite spot to go to. Where I am from, we like to sit on the front porch in the evenings. I grew up in a neighborhood that was mostly Italians. It made sense as to why I would feel at home on the front porch of a hotel that was modeled after a city in Italy.

Back in Minnesota when I had the realization that I was just existing and not truly living. Well, this is when I started living. During that time, I went to every major hotel, and experienced all I could that made Las Vegas the famous place that it is: I saw Siegfried and Roy's white tigers, and I met Mr. Las Vegas, Wayne Newton. I became a regular at comedian George Wallace's show at the West Gate Hotel, my spot was the chair in the front row to the far left. I was having the time of my life.

It was beginning to find out who I was, and I was making Las Vegas my home. All of it was great, but I decided that I needed more. That is when I decided that I needed to pay it forward. Just like I had asked Geofrey to do. That is when I started Mother Martha Family Foundation in Las Vegas.

I wanted to make sure that the work being done at Bulamu Children's Village where Geofrey and Ivan grew up continued. What Uncle Joseph started there not only saved the lives of hundreds of Ugandan children, indirectly it saved my life too.

Las Vegas wasn't for Barb. After a few months she moved back to West Virginia. Everyone has their own path in life and Vegas wasn't for her. But I was thriving there. I found my personal style in clothing, what food I liked, it was like I was discovering this entirely new person. I guess you could say I was discovering who I always was. Now I had a purpose to take all the negatives and turn them into something positive.

Chapter 10:

Journey around the world.

"Our greatest freedom is the freedom to choose our attitude.'
-Viktor W. Frankl

There I was alone in Las Vegas miles away from anyone I knew. Now I had this big goal that I was going to start a foundation to help the orphanage in Uganda. I wasn't sure how I was going to do it. All I had was the suitcase I had left West Virginia with. My thought was, Gandhi changed an entire nation, and he did not even have pants. I had pants, so no excuses. I would find a way to help the children at Bulamu.

One evening after work I made a buck list. A list of things I always wanted to but couldn't because I was held down my circumstances. It looked like this: Eat pizza in New York City, see the Eiffel Tower, eat pizza in Milan, spend time with my friend Sadat in the middle east, and go to Uganda. The end of the list was the most important. I wanted to go to Uganda to hug Geofrey for helping to save my life.

After a few months of saving some money, I took the one thing I had left from my life, that white suitcase full of essential items and boarded a plane at McCarren International Airport in Las Vegas. With that list in my hand ready to mark each one off.

I looked a bit different then compared to when I was sitting on that bench waiting for Ivan at the Minneapolis-St Paul Airport just a year earlier. Then I looked a mess, like I was dead inside, a shell of a person. Now it was like a light was shinning inside me.

My style of clothing was now designer blouses, tight jeans, and high heels. I love big earrings, sparkly jewelry. My hair went from long and brown to shoulder length and dark blonde. I found out I had a great sense of humor, and I smiled a lot. Mother Martha was no longer just existing but truly living.

First stop, New York City to eat pizza, and then to Paris France. Two items marked off my list in just a few days after leaving Las Vegas. Then my trip changed, my next flight was into the middle east. I was meeting my friend Sadat at Dubai International Airport.

Chapter 11:

A new Family Emerges.

Sadat had to leave his home quickly to save his life but for a different reason. Sadat was exiled from Uganda for speaking his mind. He could no longer deal with the oppression he saw around him. It is difficult for me to understand what it is like to live in a place where speaking your mind can get you jail time or even killed. That is the truth for people in Uganda and in many countries in the world.

Many Ugandans have told me as children they are told, "Watch what you say, the government can hear you, the walls have ears." A fear of the government is instilled in them from childhood.

Sadat's father had been a wealthy businessman in Uganda until the current leadership came into power. It is what dictators do. They take out those they feel will keep them from remaining in power. He had enough of living life under fear. As a child his father was dropping him off for school and he was shot in the leg. The bullet was intended for his father but missed him and hit eleven-year-old Sadat in the leg. The authorities came to arrest the rest of his family. His younger sister lost her life, her body was found in the dust bin not long after the arrest. In Uganda, a dust bin is the area where the trash is taken out. Her body was disposed of like a bag of trash as if she were not human.

Sadat's father was arrested by the government and never seen again after his arrest. All the wealth his father had accumulated was taken and he was arrested. No one heard or saw his father again after his arrest. His mother and grandmother raised the children on what they had left they best they could.

Sadat was tired of the state of his country, so he began to speak his mind. Men broke into his home and there was a failed attempt to kill him. Just like me, he ran with few belongings. He went where he knew people and where he could make a fresh start. He started a charitable foundation in Uganda to help children while he was living in Dubai. That is how we became friends; we both love children and have a passion for helping in Uganda.

I will never forget landing in Dubai. After living in Las Vegas, it was a culture shock for me. I believe in understanding the culture and laws of any country before planning to visit. Respecting the beliefs and emotions of others is a priority for me. This was the first time wearing a hijab, and I had to ask for assistance from another passenger on the plane to put it on.

The culture change began in the airport—the Arabic writing on the signs, the modest clothing, and the music playing overhead.

The sight of Sadat caught my eye as I scanned the crowd of people—he was the only person not dressed in traditional Islamic wear. Knowing it was against the law, I resisted the urge to hug him when he approached me.

Sadat and I are about the same height, he is slinder with long arms and legs. Dark complexion, big rounded brown eyes, small ears, his accent is different than Ivan's or Geofrey's. I assumed he was from a different region of Uganda. I am from the southeast United States, I have a what is considered a "Southern accent." We exchanged pleasantries and walked to his car in the passenger pickup area.

The sights of downtown Dubai were amazing to me. Not like the bright lights of Las Vegas but magnificent just the same. When we were in the car, I was looking out the windows more than talking to my friend. Which might have come off as rude. I lost the ability to see the world around me after the car accident but once I regained it, I swore I never want to take for granted again.

A wonderful mixture of large skyscrapers, beaches, tourist, and Arabian flair. I was impressed at first sight. Sadat began to point out the different landmarks as we drove past them—Burj Al Arab, the Dubai Mall, and the Dubai fountains. He dropped me off at my hotel to give me time to rest. I had just traveled across five time zones, and it was not easy on a body as beat up as mine.

Sadat picked me up a few hours later. He was going to show me Dubai, his version of Dubai. I like to explore places with people that live there, I think you get a more authentic experience. Sadat was my friend; we had a lot of catching up to do. He decided to take me to an American restaurant. Not sure why since I live in the United States. But it was interesting to taste American food in the middle east. I love to try new foods, he promised to take me for traditional food of the area the next time.

I like to laugh and tell jokes. My laugh is loud and unique. Sadat had to tell me many times to please lower my voice. But in his defense sometimes people must tell me that in the United States as well. We sat and talked about his work in Uganda with orphans. I shared with him what I planned to do in the future with Mother Martha Family Foundation.

Sadat is a gentleman. He conducts himself in such a way that makes you feel he has it all together. He looked handsome in his grey suit, and blue tie. He clearly came to impress. If he was flirting with me, I did not notice. I was jet-lagged and not looking to date anyone. I was there to spend time with my friend and talk about how we can help children in Uganda.

After eating, we decided to take a walk. I agreed because it seemed like such a beautiful city from the car, I figured on foot it would be much more impressive. I put on my purple hijab to prepare to walk the city. Sadat informed me that in the tourist areas such as the spice market, the gold market, I did not need to wear it.

One thing that stood out to me was that people were walking cats on leashes like people would walk their dogs in the evening in the United States. I turned to Sadat and said, "Are they walking cats?"

Sadat grinned and said "Yes they are walking their house cats" as if he did not find it odd.

I said, "Well Darlin', where I come from our cats stay in the house, if they go outside, we just open the door and let them go outside. We walk our dogs like that." To him that seemed a little odd.

I said, "How do you get a cat on a leash? The cat I had for years was grumpy. He scratched and fought me just putting a collar around his neck."

We both laughed as we continued walking.

Sadat stated that he was tired and ready to go home for the night. He decided he would hail a cab for me to take back to my hotel. He stepped out to the curb to hail a cab with no response for a while. It seemed odd to me. But I had been there for less than 24 hours maybe it was not odd for Dubai. It was completely different than what I was used to back in the states. After he tried for several minutes, a cab stopped. The driver got out, stood next to his car then lit a cigarette. He approached us quickly speaking in a language I assumed was Arabic. A look of anger on his face. Human emotions are recognizable across all cultures.

Sadat grabbed me by the arm and said, "Let's go" in a forceful tone. We started walking away quickly.

After we walked for several minutes that way, I stopped and said, "What was that guy's problem?"

Sadat turned to me and said, "Martha, he is an ignorant man. He refused to give us a ride because you are a white woman with an African man." Since my hotel was not far from there, we decided that we would just continue to walk. We agreed that I just had two more days there and much more to see that we would rest as to get an early start in the morning.

We spend the next two days going to the tourist sites. It was a great to experience the culture. I did get to try the local food. At the end of my visit, I knew I had made an ally in what I wanted to do for the orphanage. As I boarded the plane in Dubai for Uganda, I felt a sadness in my heart leaving Sadat. I enjoyed my time in Dubai. I learned a lot about the culture and the people. I got closer to my friend. I knew I would be packing my suitcase to visit Dubai again.

Then a wave of excitement came over me with the thought that in just six hours, I would be in Uganda with Geofrey. Geofrey and I continued to talk while I was in Minnesota and Las Vegas. We talked less than we did before because we both just became busier. He was running AMKA Foundation Africa and I was making a new life in Las Vegas.

Chapter 12:

Welcome to the Pearl of Africa.

> "Life ultimately means taking the responsibility to find the right answers to it problems."
> -Viktor E. Frankl

I was told a lot of stories about what life was like in Uganda. Winston Churchill called it the pearl of Africa. I was full of excitement and anticipation to see Uganda and wrap my arms around Geofrey.

Six hours later, I looked out the window of the plane at Entebbe, Uganda. The beautiful landscape around Lake Victoria is stunning—small huts with children playing outside, farm animals and fishing boats on the water.

As they announced our landing in twenty minutes at Entebbe International Airport my anticipation grew. I had traveled 10,000 miles. Although I was feeling jet lagged nothing could lesson my feelings of excitement.

I stepped onto the stairs to exit the plane, I looked around with amazement. I could not believe I was in Uganda. As soon as I saw the airport, I said out loud 'That looks like my grandfather's chicken coup back in West Virginia." We were directed through a building and put in line that had a sign that said immigration at the end. We were told to have our documents ready to enter in the country.

I had been living the past year in Las Vegas, just visited some of the historical sites in the world. The first 10 minutes into my visit in Uganda was already a shock. After going through the line, I asked where I pick my suitcase. The man pointed to the right of him, the one run down looking baggage claim terminal they had. I exchanged some of my United States dollars for Ugandan shillings. Then went out to the passenger pick up area.

I walked out to see a group of people rushing around and there was so much background noise it was an assault to the senses. The roads were dust, with big mud holes. It was muggy hot, which I expected being East Africa. I was looking for Geofrey in this big crowd of people. I figured if I stand still then they would see me. I was the only white person around as far as I could see.

I has I stood that I thought about how many twists and turns in my life have happened at airports. As I looked around my heart was racing with anticipation. A few minutes later Geofrey stepped out of the crowd. I dropped everything, and I ran to him. I threw my arms around him. He threw his arms around me. Tears of joy came down my face. It was like time stood still. Noise of the people rushing around us continued but for us it seemed as though time stood still. I could not let go. I did not want to let go.

After a few minutes Francis, Geofrey's best friend, came forward and tapped us on the shoulder. He said, "Okay, you two. Our ride is here. We must get Martha to her hotel in Entebbe."

Still not wanting to let go of Geofrey I picked up my suitcase and held his hand. Geofrey looked at me and spoke for the first time, "I cannot believe you are here!"

I stated, "I certainly cannot believe I am here, but I am grateful."

Francis took my suitcase to load in his car. I was still holding onto Geofrey's hand as we walked to the car. Geofrey looks much like his brother Ivan. Tall and slender. Geofrey has much bigger ears and is a little taller. Ivan is introvert than rarely leaves his apartment, but Geofrey is more of social person. Social but a bit of an intellectual. We were both had smiles on our faces when we got into Francis's car.

The drive from the airport to my hotel I was taking in the scenery of Uganda. It is like God painted this picture just for us. Untouched by humans in many places. It was more amazing than I had ever imagined it would be. Beautiful trees, greenery, and the sky a beautiful clear blue.

The areas where people lived were the opposite of anything in Las Vegas. Dirt roads, women carrying baskets on their heads, and many people driving motorcycles. Not just one person or two people on a motorcycle but up to five people on some motorcycles. Many of them were children with no helmets. As a nurse, I was horrified. I wanted Francis to stop the car so I could get out and say, "Be safe! Put helmets on, put helmets on those children!" I guess that is why I got the nickname Momma Martha, always mothering everyone. Francis said, "Those are called Boda Bodas here."

My friendship with Francis was different than the mother/son type relationship I had with Geofrey. Francis and I like to tell each other jokes. I said, "Whatever they are called they are unsafe, and I want to get out and enforce safety rules."

Everyone in the car began to laugh at me trying to be a mother to the entire town of Entebbe.

We pulled into the driveway at Frontier Hotel, less than a half of a mile to the State House of Uganda, and a view of Lake Victoria. It is a small hotel with walls around the boarder of the property made of blocks with barbed wire on the top. At the beginning of the driveway is a guard house before you get to the entrance of the hotel.

The landscape is typical of East Africa—tropical trees, and green grass. I knew when I stepped out of the car and saw the pizza place on the grounds of the hotel that this was my place. After checking into the hotel, we all agreed I should rest. The following day was already packed with activities.

Jet lag was starting to affect me: headache, fatigue, and upset stomach. I gave Geofrey a hug goodbye. For Francis, it was one of our silly jokes, and a "see you tomorrow."

I sat my suitcase on the bed and went to the sliding glass doors, that lead to the balcony. As I moved the curtain to the side the view of Lake Victoria revealed itself. As I walked out on the balcony to get a better view, what I saw I can only describe as the most magnificent view I have ever seen.

Birds were chirping, the sounds from the farm animals close by, and the sights and sounds of the monkeys playing in the trees. The sun was setting over the lake. At that moment, I forgot about being jetlagged, my heart was at peace. The best way to describe it is that it was a feeling of, "I am home." That's when I realized why Winston Churchill called Uganda the pearl of Africa. The shores of Lake Victoria left a lasting imprint on my heart that day.

The room was basic, the floor was tile, the bed linens had elephants and giraffes on them. On the side was a desk with an outdated computer on it. There was a television mounted on the wall. Big closets to the side. There was an air conditioner—one of those small units—which worked quite well.

The bathroom had an open shower and a small sink. I liked that there was a skylight so that the African sun can shine in on you as you shower.

I prepared for bed that night, I began to wonder how such a beautiful place could have the problems they have. Many children in orphanages. Then thought of seeing Zaake Francis being hit in the head with a chair on the floor of parliament started to play in my mind. I was excited to see more of Uganda. I put the mosquito net over me in bed, and quickly fell asleep.

Waking up to the sounds of Lake Victoria, I quickly got out of bed with excitement. I was going to see AMKA Foundation Africa. I got dressed and went down to the restaurant for breakfast.

A spread of fresh fruits, and breads was sitting out on a table to the side of the sitting area. As I sat down a very well-dressed young lady came out of the kitchen and asked me if I wanted an omelet for breakfast. Since I had seen chickens on the property the evening before my answer was an immediate, "Yes please."

When the young lady brought the omelet to the table, I asked her if she knew of any drivers that could drive me to Kampala this morning on short notice. The distance from Entebbe to Kampala they said was about 54 km. I had no idea how far that was since we don't use the metric system in the United States.

Regina, the young lady I meet working the front desk, came to tell me that Kampala was a fifty-minute drive away and that they would call Sam, a driver that she knew well. She stated, "Sam lives not far from here in Entebbe and he might be able to drive you on short notice."

Just thirty minutes later a very tall, muscular young man walked into the restaurant introducing himself as Sam. That he was there to drive me to Kampala. The accents of people in Uganda make everything they say sound so proper to me. Until 1962, Uganda was under the rule of the British, so they speak the Queen's English. I sound more like Paula Dean, the TV cook from the southeast United States.

We agreed on a price for him to be my driver for the day. After I finished my omelet, we set off for AMKA Foundation Africa.

AMKA gives young people job skills, they teach hair dressing, cosmetology, computer operation, and fashion design courses. Geofrey came up with the idea for the fashion design course from the stories I used to tell him about my neighbor, Camilla. She taught me how to sew and make my own clothes as a teenager. My parents were factory workers in West Virginia when I was growing up. We did not have the money for me to dress like the popular girls at school. But with Camilla's help, I looked just as good as them.

In the parking lot of Frontier Hotel, Sam opened the back door of a late model Toyota. When I got in the car, the first thing I noticed was a piece of cloth that looked like fur covering the dashboard. He got in the driver's seat on the right, which to me was the wrong side.

When I inquired about the fur on his dashboard Sam stated it was there to cut down on the dust. I said, "Makes sense because of the dirt roads." Then I began to look out of the windows as we pulled past the guard house coming out of the hotel driveway.

Sam reached up and pushed a button on the radio. The familiar sound of Dolly Parton's song "Coat of Many Colors" got my attention.

I said, "Do you like Dolly Parton's music?"

Sam said, "Ms. Parton is one the most popular singers in Uganda."

I leaned forward toward the front seat with a look of shock on my face. "Really?" I said with surprise in my voice.

Sam said, "The song 'When I think About Love' is the most played love song in Uganda. It is played at weddings, dances, and anywhere there are lovers." I said, "That is amazing. I grew up on Dolly Parton's music. Hmm…it really is a small world. Well, then let's enjoy some Dolly on the way to AMKA." We played our favorite Dolly Parton music for the hour trip to AMKA as I looked out the window enjoying the scenery.

Sam and I talked periodically along the way—the usual getting to know you type stuff, where did you grow up, and how is your family. After just an hour of talking to this man I had just met, I had learned that we had a lot in common. He had lived in Dubai, and I had just come from that area. We discussed what we had both experienced there. We liked the same movies, music, and traveling. He was happy in a relationship with a young lady named Brenda. That was where our commonalities ended. I told him briefly about my love life and that subject ended with the statement, "I have no desire to date." He said, "Okay," with a look on his face like he was thinking, we will not go there with that subject of conversation.

We pulled into a neighborhood in Kampala about an hour later. It was the poorest neighborhood I had ever seen—dirt roads, dwellings made of cardboard with tin roofs. There were slabs of meat just hanging outside with flies swarming them. Children played around the dwellings with holes in their clothing. It was a sight I was not prepared for. At that moment I remembered to check to see if I had taken my daily dose of the malaria prevention medication my doctor back in Las Vegas.

Female mosquitoes are the deadliest animals on the planet and malaria is a major problem in Uganda. I will never forget the sight of that neighborhood. Geofrey said he started AMKA Foundation there because it was where the need was the greatest. Now that I was seeing it, I understood why he picked this neighborhood.

Sam pulled in front of an entrance in front of a big wooden door. Block fences and security doors are the normal in Uganda, so the large security door was not alarming to me. A young man came to the door and swung it open. The sign to AMKA was large outside an orange building. I was feeling a little anxious to meet everyone. A group of young ladies greeted me after I got out of the car carrying a big bouquet of orange flowers. Orange was the color that Geofrey had chosen for AMKA uniforms. He chose that color because my mentor that had passed on a few years earlier loved orange. Seeing those young ladies looking so beautiful in their uniforms made me smile thinking of my mentor. The wisdom she passed down to me was worth more than any gold in the world. The students wearing her color felt like it was a sort of in remembrance of her to me.

I took the flowers from students as they said, "Welcome." I did not know if it would be proper to hug them or even if they could speak English. I thought education might be an issue here, but the assumption was based on what I had seen on the way there.

Geofrey comes out the front door of AMKA and hugs me. He states, "Everyone speaks English, Momma Martha." He must have seen the puzzled look on my face. A little boy who looked about four years old came running to me. Then stopped and looked up as if he were surprised. Geofrey said, "I think this is the first time he has ever seen a white person." It honestly never entered my mind that someone there may have never seen a white person before. I had always lived in the United States, we are a country of people of many races and cultures.

He spoke to Geofrey in a language I did not understand. He asked Geofrey if I was an angel or a devil. It did not bother me. After all he was seeing someone that looked different than him for the first time. I put down the flowers and smiled at him, reaching out my arms as if to hug him—a gesture anyone can understand no matter race, culture, or language. The next thing I knew that young man was in my arms, and I was carrying him around. I quickly figured out I was not a devil.

That is when I learned the word Mzungu. It is not a term of racism. Mzungu literally translates to mean "foreigner." It is just a matter-of-fact description to say the person has light skin or the person is not of African heritage.

Geofrey lead me to the area where the fashion design course was being taught. He introduced me to Ruth, the teacher of that course. I had recognized her from the pictures that Geofrey had sent me. Everyone at AMKA looked young, but Uganda is a country in which 70% of the population is under the age of thirty-five. Ruth showed me how she taught the students to sew before they even used any material. The cloth is expensive, so she taught them to sew with thick paper first before cutting or sewing cloth. They had seven sewing machines and thirty students, but they were making do with what they had.

The ladies at AMKA in the hairdressing course wanted to style my hair. I understood the curiosity, my hair being a different texture. I welcomed it because my hair was frizzy from the humidity. The hair styles there are amazing to me, the different braids, and the sparkly hair barrettes in their hair. The women in their culture seemed to support each other more than what I am used to in the United States.

Women in the United States can be very catty and mean to each other. In the southeast, if someone says, "Bless your heart," honey, they are not really trying to bless you. It is a passive-aggressive insult.

Francis came out to the class and ushered me down a small hallway into a small office. It had a desk and a living room furniture set up. I sat down in a big fluffy couch that I seem to sink into. Francis and Geofrey wanted to share with me what AMKA had been doing since its start in December 2017.

It was amazing to me how many people's lives were positively affected. I proudly looked out at Francis and Geofrey has they talked about the students of AMKA past and present. They talked about their plans to add more classes such as auto repair and welding. They needed more computers for the computer class. They asked the students to pay it forward after they graduated from their classes. By then they had graduated three classes since each course is six months long. Asking the students to pay it forward led to one student coming back to teach classes.

I was overwhelmed with emotion. All of it had began because of one kind act I did a few years earlier. At that moment I was proud of Geofrey and evreryone at AMKA.

That evening I said goodbye to everyone as I got into Sam's car to return to Entebbe. It was clear to me that Uganda had more problems than I imagined. I glad that AMKA was doing its part no matter how small to help people find solutions.

Chapter 13:

Visiting Bulamu where Geofrey grew up was a real eye opener.

"Success like happiness, is the unexpected side effect of one's personal dedication to a cause greater than oneself."
-Viktor E. Frankl

Sam agreed to drive me to Bulamu Children's Village the next day. Driving in Uganda is an experience that can only be described as I feel like we are in an action movie. There are no traffic lights, no traffic lanes, no street signs, and hundreds of boda bodas going in every direction. Sometimes the Boda Bodas are weighed down carrying supplies. Cars and vans going in different directions. Totally chaotic yet somehow people get to where they are going. It just became a joke between us that when we got to Kampala I would say, "Its just like an action movie, Jason Borne as nothing on us."

The drive to Bulamu seemed to take several hours. I learned by then that Dolly Parton music was always on standby in his car.

After what seemed like an hour we drove into area where there were many small houses in looked like the middle of nowhere. We pulled into a driveway where a big wooden door opened as we pulled into the driveway, much like the door at AMKA foundation. As the gates opened, I could see children to our left playing soccer in a field, it is called football there.

I was eager to see where Geofrey had talked to me from all those years. As I got out of Sam's car a flood of memories entered my mind of the stories, he had told me about his life here. Then I thought about how much different Geofrey and I were right then compared to when he was talking to me from here. Back then he was an orphan, and I was an abused woman in West Virginia. I was of proud of the progress we both had made. How much we had learned and grown as people.

Children were playing around us but not paying us much mind. A man approached us who I recognized as Joseph Lubega, the man everyone lovingly calls "Uncle Joseph", approached us. He is the founder of Bulamu Children's Village. He is a very respected man in his community, rightfully so because what he has done has positively affected thousands of people including me. As we stood there shaking hands, there were almost nine hundred children residing at Bulamu. He had already raised a generation of children that included Ivan and Geofrey. Uncle Joseph was taller than I expected. When he shook my hand, I felt I was in the presence of a strong but kind person. Not many people master of the art of being soft and strong. To me I was shaking the hand of an angel on Earth. Because of the character and values he had instilled in Ivan and Geofrey, I was still alive. I loved him as family at first sight. That is when he became my Uncle Joseph as well.

"Welcome, sister Martha," Joseph said with a smile.

I awkwardly reached out my arms to give him a big hug. After all, his actions did help to save my life in the big picture. After the awkward hug I introduced Uncle Joseph to Sam. We began to walk around Bulamu as we talked.

I was not prepared for what I saw next. I knew from Geofrey's stories that people were trying their best to help with what resources they have. What I imagined it to be, from my American perspective, was much better than what I saw that day. Geofrey had downplayed what he saw. He was telling me from a perspective of a young man that had lost his parents and was probably just grateful that he and Ivan were not homeless on the streets anymore.

The school rooms were just bare floors—no desks, no books, no paper, no pencils, and just a chalkboard on the walls. Unlike in the US where tax dollars pay for public school, parents must pay to educate their children. We were then directed outside to walk toward the children's sleeping area. As I turned my head, I felt a tug on my pant leg. I look down to see a little girl. She looked to be about four to five years old. She had no hair and was wearing an orange dress. I knew she was malnourished based on her appearance. As a nurse, I had seen it enough to know.

"Hello, young lady," I said. She did not speak back. I did not pay attention to it at first. Maybe she just did not know English. She reached up to me and I reached out my hand, and we began to walk hand in hand together.

Uncle Joseph turned to me. "I see you have met Catherine."

"Indeed, I just made a new friend," I stated with a smile on my face. Catherine and I followed beside Uncle Joseph hand in hand as he continued his tour.

As we walked to the sleeping area, I saw mattresses piled up outside the small houses we had seen from the entrance of Bulamu. Sam turned to asked why the mattresses were placed there. Uncle Joseph plainly stated that during rainy season the water gets inside the houses. The mattress become wet, and the children must place them outside in the sun to dry.

I looked up at Uncle Joseph's face and said, "This is where Geofrey was talking to me from?"

"Not this particular house, but yes, one near this one," stated Joseph.

Tears began to flow down my face.

This was worse than what I had imagined it would be. After seeing the sights here and the day before, the conditions around AMKA Foundation Africa, I started to wonder how these things can happen. I knew the answer probably lay in poor leadership and greed. Putting money before human lives is the root of many problems in the world.

Putting money first and the lives of people second is something I never understood. Seems to me that money comes from people, through buying goods and services that keep economies going. One of my favorite authors, Zig Ziglar, used to say, "You can have everything you want in life by helping others get what they want." He meant that by solving people's problems through goods and services you will have abundance.

Anything can be used for construction or destruction depending on the person's character that is directing it. Money, just like anything else, can be used for good—to build a business, help a friend, or take your date out to a nice dinner. It can used for destructive purposes. No need to list those. During my visit in Uganda, I had not seen much construction yet a lot of destruction.

With a quiver in my voice, I asked, "So tell me how the children get dressed in the mornings. Where are their clothes, and who helps the little ones?" I said as a bit of a joke, "I know one man does not help four hundred children get ready for school in the mornings. Just getting one up and going is quite a chore."

Everyone laughed. "There are house mothers in each house. They help the children in that house prepare for the day. We pay teachers to come into the classrooms to teach. For each child we try to get them sponsors to help purchase the necessary books, uniforms, and school supplies."

We then walked to the garden area where the children learned to grow food. It was located behind the living area. Uncle Joseph said feeding the children was the most challenging part of it all. That is when he showed us the area where the children eat, that is when Catherine finally let go of my hand to eat her lunch. The area where the children eat is basically a spot on the ground. They get their food on plates and then find a spot to sit on the ground.

All the stories that Geofrey told me about growing up here came flooding back. He talked frequently of going to bed on an empty stomach. Sleeping in a bed with five other children. Despite that, I knew Uncle Joseph and the adults at Bulamu were doing the best they could for the four hundred children they had in their care.

After eating, the children attended church. Sam and I attended with them that day. Most of the church services were in Luganda, one of the local languages. Sam was kind enough to interrupt for me. Catherine found me in the pews, sat in my lap and then fell asleep. We spent the rest of the evening socializing with the children and staff at Bulamu.

I mixed emotions at the end of my visit. It left a sadness in my heart to see how the children were living. But it was also heartwarming to see how people were trying their best to help them. The heart of the people there and love they had for those children is amazing.

My passion had grown to help those children. I had found purpose and meaning and what I had went through, I wanted to ensure that working happening at Bulamu Children's Village continued. I wasn't sure how I was going to do it, but I was more determined than before.

As Sam and I were pulling out of the driveway to begin our journey back to Entebbe down that country road that reminded me of my home in West Virginia. I was grateful for my friendship with Geofrey. Through our friendship and connection, we had helped each other to heal. I was grateful for the new family and purpose I now had in my life.

Chapter 14:

A date with a Prince.

> "Live as if you were living a second time,
> and as though you acted wrongly the first time."
> -Viktor E. Frankl

Up until this time I had not really examined how I felt about men and the subject of dating. I pretty much avoided the matter. As far as platonic relationships, a new family had come into my life made up of mostly men: Joe, Ivan, Geofrey, Sam. They had taught me a lot about myself and how women should be treated. I was respected as "Mother Martha."

Looking back at it all, I was grateful for what I happened. I was stronger and wiser for it all. I knew what I wanted in a relationship, and I knew what I did not want. But I wasn't sure if was ready to start dating again.

Sam decided to stay my driver for the rest of my trip in Uganda. I had seen Bulamu and AMKA but I still had some things to do. After a day of rest, Sam drove me to Mengo palace in Kamapala, Uganda. Edward Mutesa was the first President of Uganda and the King of the Buganda Kingdom. Like me he was forced to run for his life from his home. Although the similarities in our stories stopped, I felt a connection to King Mutesa. I wanted to know more about his story.

I had become friends with his grandson Prince Walugembe through trying to get Mother Martha Family Foundation started. He invited to me to tour Mengo palace, the home his grandfather was exiled from.

As I stood there looking at the clothing hanging in the closet of my hotel room that I brought from Las Vegas, I thought, what does a Las Vegas girl wear to a palace to meet an African Prince? At that moment I realized how weird and wonderful my life had truly become—I was going to meet a Prince! I decided to dress just as I would in Las Vegas. I would show up as me, the person I had become after all the tragedy. High heels, blue jeans, and a designer blouse. They invited me so I was going to attend as "Mother Martha."

Sam picked me up in the front reception area as usual and to the chaotic traffic of Kampala we went once again. We approached an entrance unlike the ones that I had seen in other places in Uganda. When I asked about it, he said that it was the entrance to the palace for the reigning king of the Buganda Kingdom. The king is not allowed to go in circles, he is only allowed to go straight. This straight entrance was only for him. It seemed odd to me yet fascinating at the same time.

I said to Sam, "Darlin', I live in Las Vegas the only king we know is Elvis. The king of rock in roll."

We both laughed out loud as we drove the circle around the king's entrance.

We parked in a parking lot of what looked like an office building. The building looked like it was built in the 1960s. Many places in

Uganda look as though they are stuck in a time warp. Because the last progressive leadership it had was in the 1960s, at least that is the way it seemed to me.

Fredrick had given us specific directions for when we arrived. First, to go to the reception area on the third floor and ask for him. He said, "Tell them that I am expecting you at 11:00 am to tour Mengo palace."

We went to the third floor and asked for Prince Fredrick as he instructed. The receptionist asked us to take a seat in the reception area of the offices of the radio station and television station of the Buganda Kingdom. I barely recognize celebrities in the US, so I knew I would not recognize the celebrities of Uganda. The king himself could have come walking by, I would have not known who he was. But when Prince Fredrick entered the room, I knew who he was immediately. He looks just like his grandfather. If a movie is ever made about Edward Mutesa, his grandson is his twin. Killer smile, slim build, and dressed in a black suit and tie. He looked very handsome, just as you would imagine an African Prince.

He approached me and said, "Hello Martha, Welcome to the Buganda Kingdom," in his very proper British accent.

I said "Nice to meet you, Frederick. This is my friend Sam."

Fredrick and Sam shook hands and they began the get to know you type conversation, nice to meet you, where are you from type stuff. Prince Fredrick then said "Let's walk this way, we will begin our tour with the radio station and the television station then go to the palace.

We walked to the first floor of the building to the radio station. He showed us where the most popular radio shows are recorded. While inside an empty studio we saw a record player, I was the only one who remembered when people had them. A pleasant memory of my grandmother came to me—of my grandmother playing Kenny Rogers records in our living room. I met so many people during the tour of the radio station CBS FM, that I could not remember their names. But everyone was friendly and accommodating.

Prince Fredrick then led us into a building next door, to BBS the kingdom's television station. He introduced me to the station manager. That gentleman took us into a studio where the most popular comedy show was being filmed. The actors were speaking Luganda, I could not understand what they were saying but I was grateful for the experience.

We then exited the building to an outside veranda. It was large and on the left was a big tent set up with a big group of people underneath it. Sam had said he needed to use the bathroom, so we stopped for a moment, leaving me alone with Prince Fredrick.

There was a moment of silence then he said, "I cannot believe you are here all the way from Las Vegas."

I said, "Well doll, you know my story and what Ivan and Geofrey did for me." Prince Fredrick nodded his head and smiled.

Then he did something I never expected—he leaned forward to kiss me. I did not fight it. A handsome Prince with a killer smile comes forward to kiss you, you kiss him back. Besides, I had not dated since I left my previous relationship. The thought really did not cross my mind. But it was on my mind as Prince Fredrick pressed his lips against mine. He then put his arm around my waist and pulled my body close to his. Just then in that moment Sam came out to find us. We awkwardly pulled away from each other trying to pretend nothing had happened.

Fredrick grabbed my hand. "Now come over here and let's take our picture in front of the statute of King Mutebi, my uncle."

Sam was just looking over at me as if he were holding back teasing me about the kiss he had accidentally witnessed as he took a picture of us. After taking our picture in front of the statue of the King, I noticed on our left were tents with a large amount of people sitting in chairs. It looked like a party. People were happy and dressed in beautiful clothing, it was all very colorful and festive.

Fredrick then turned his head toward Sam and I. "To our left is where people from the kingdom come every Wednesday to bring a gift to the King. To the front of us is the mile of road that on each side is a piece of land where each clan within the kingdom has placed things that represent their clan. It is called the Royal Mile." Fredrick turned to Sam and asked, "Can you please go get the car? Bring it around so we can drive down the royal mile to Mengo palace."

This was when I really began to have a real interest in our tour. The kiss from the handsome Prince was good, but I was eager to see where Edward Mutesa had to flee from to save his life. I had lived through the same not long ago, so I felt a connection to his story. A person can understand how something feels when they have experienced it for themselves.

Having to run out of primal fear, not knowing where you can go and not knowing who you can trust with your life. At times not knowing where you next meal with come from or where you will lay your head down at night. It is an experience I do not wish on anyone. Not even those who caused it for me.

Sam pulled around the car, and Prince Fredrick and I got in the backseat. We were leaving the administration building of the kingdom and then began driving what Prince Fredrick identified as "the royal mile"—a mile of road that stretches between the kingdom administration building to Mengo palace. Along this mile of road each of the fifty-two clans that make up the Buganda Kingdom have a totem on a plot of land. Each totem represents their clan, such as there is a monkey clan.

Prince Fredrick pointed to a small plot of land with a statue of a monkey on it with beautiful trees surrounding it. "Each person in the Kingdom when they say their names, we can tell which clan they are from. It is frowned upon for people to marry from within their own clan, the forefathers knew that DNA should not be mixed within the clans."

Sam pulled in a small parking lot. We got out of the car to an entry way that had a statue of a lion on either side. What you would expect the entry way of a royal palace in east Africa to look like. It was quite an amazing sight. There were two gentlemen dressed in uniforms who greeted us speaking Luganda, I assumed they were palace guards. After they were done speaking to Prince Fredrick, the big entry way doors opened. As they opened, they revealed Mengo palace. It was not what I had expected. I guess Hollywood movies had put bigger expectations in my mind. But it was still magnificent in its own way.

It was big yellow building that looked like it was built in the 1960s. Beautiful with a quite regal feeling to it. The landscape around it was typical of that area. It looked like what you would think the garden of Eden looked like. The two men directed us to the right into a small building. As I entered, a young lady came forward to say that it was tradition for ladies to wear a dress on the palace grounds. I had dressed for my visit to the palace like I dress in Las Vegas. When Prince Fredrick invited me, he got me. But I understood traditions were necessary to follow. The young lady began to put a very colorful skirt around my waist. When she was done, I felt like a princess.

A man palace greeted us and introduced himself as a palace guide. I was eager to learn about King Edward Mutesa II. Sam, Fredrick, the palace guide, and I walked to the entrance of the palace. Fredrick directed me to sit down with him on the stairs in front of the palace. We laughed together as we sat for pictures. After we posed for the camera the tour guide stated that we could not go inside certain places in the palace without the King's permission. Which was fine with me, I was there for him to tell me King Mutesa's story.

We began to walk around the palace grounds. The guide pointed to a spot at the palace wall where Mutesa has ran for his life and had to jump the wall for his safety. I understood the feeling of having to leave your home in a hurry and not being able to turn back. He went to England during his exile. His life story included the

Queen of England, the Pope, and world leaders. My story was not similar in that way. I did not grow up royalty—my parents were factory workers from West Virginia. I am from a different culture, continent, and country. But I could understand what it felt like for him to have to run for his life.

We continued to walk past a couple of run-down buildings. There were chickens, and a few children playing in the front. The scenery took a turn from the beauty that surrounded the palace. From bright, beautiful, picturesque landscape to dark, and run down. The palace guide said that these some of the first buildings built there on that property. They were keeping them in their original state. I found it sad, and I waved at the little girl playing on the ground outside of one of those little rundown buildings. The guide pointed ahead said that the torture chambers of Idi Admin were just ahead.

Idi Admin was a former President of Uganda and one of the people that exiled King Mutesa. In the United States there was a movie made surrounding Iddi Amin in 2006. His role was portrayed by actor Forrest Whitaker. I started to wonder why there was never a movie made about him who was the King, first President and a decorated military man who was Knighted by the Queen of England. I guess movies about bad guys sells more tickets.

I began to feel cold as we approached the torture chambers. A sense of sadness filled my body. Fredrick must have noticed the sadness on my face—he put his arm around me to comfort me. They are chambers that are underground. The feeling of sadness began when I saw the sign to the right of the entrance of the chambers. The sign states: Welcome to the Iddi Amin's Armory that was constructed by the Israeli in the early 1970s but later turned into a torture chamber where thousands of Ugandans lost their lives.

The palace guide began to tell me the story of what happened in Amin's torture chambers. People who were considered enemies of the state were taken there to be tortured. First, they were put in cars and driven around Kampala so that they would not know where they were located when they got out of the car. On the walls were messages written in blood. The tortured souls used their blood to write on the walls what their tormentors did to them. Tears began to fill my eyes at the sight of those bloody messages on the walls.

The chambers above a pit of water with electricity running through it. If the prisoners jumped, they were jumping to their deaths. Sometimes up to twenty people a day lost their lives here. The sight in front of me was the work of Edward Mutesa's enemies—brutal, evil killers. If you had disagreed with them this was your fate.

When then began walking to toward an area with trees and a beautiful lake in the background. He then began to tell us about the types of trees at the palace, one that bears a fruit called jackfruit. I was glad for the change of scenery. He pointed out "the Kabaka's Lake." It is a large manmade lake that was dug by hand in 1886 for King Mwanga. He had it built for an escape route during times of war. The entire place was amazingly beautiful but rooted in a bloody, brutal history.

As we walked the palace grounds the guide ended our tour at the same small building where we started. I changed back into the clothing I had arrived in that morning. As I changed my clothes back into "Mother Martha" I still felt like a princess.

As we parted ways, Fredrick asked if he could see me again before I left Uganda. I had never thought about dating before then. Maybe it was the magical feeling of where we were, but I said "yes" to a date with the handsome Prince. Sam and I pulled out of the palace driveway, down the royal mile once again and back on the road to Entebbe to my hotel.

That evening as I was getting ready for bed that night, that is when I knew I had to examine how I felt about romantic relationships. Until that time men in my life had been abusive in some way. My father was an alcoholic and verbally abusive. I could never do anything right. When he drank, he really bad-mouthed women. After a couple of beers, he would begin to pick on my mother. I learned to stand up to him at an early age. My brother was thirteen years older than me, so he was not around much. My ex-husband never had anything good to say to me or about me. I realized men had not left a good impression on me.

Because of those experiences, I knew what I did not want and what I did want in a relationship. I was stronger and wiser because of it all. In fact, I was grateful for it all. Not only was I now strong enough to stand up for myself, but I was strong enough to stand up for others. I felt I was ready to start dating again. Which was good because I had just made a date with a Prince!

Chapter 15:

Then there was danger.

"Decisions, not conditions, Determine What a Man is."
-Viktor E. Frankl

I had just been in Uganda under a week and already had an action filled visit. I wanted to see the source of the Nile River. It was just a two-hour drive from my hotel in Entebbe. Sam and I picked up Geofrey for the trip.

Two-hour trip driving in the landscape side of Uganda, the landscape looks much like West Virginia. Green grass, rolling hills, and farms. The difference there is that are a lot of sugar cane fields. We stopped in a village to eat at a restaurant.

That experience really opened to my perception to what life is like in villages there. The restaurant was just a hut on the side of the road. There was a piece of cloth used a front door. When we pulled back the cloth it was old wooden tables with benches. We sat down at the first table, when the waitress came Geofrey ordered for me. I had no idea what the words on the menu meant.

When my food was served, I looked around the table at Sam and Geofrey to see they were staring at me. I figured since I had an audience, I had better start eating. I found the food to be bland, but I was good. I wanted to see the kitchen. I was curious as to how food was prepared in such a hut.

Geofrey asked that waitress if I could see the kitchen and she agreed. I walked through a small doorway and saw that they were cooking on an open fire. There was an older woman on her hands and knees cleaning the floor with a scrub brush. The woman had burn scars up her arms.

I had spent that last year eating in the most famous restaurants in Las Vegas. A much different place that what I was seeing in front of me. It made me feel sad for the people of the Village. Electricity and necessities were not easy for them to obtain. It made me feel grateful for what I had experienced in Las Vegas.

An hour later we were Jinja, Uganda where the source of the Nile River is located. We parked and began walking down wooden stairs. Along the way were vendors selling their hand made arts and crafts. With each stop down we could see more of the Nile. As we got to the bottom, I saw a memorial to Gandhi. I had to pay my respects to Gandhi. He inspired me to have the courage to take on such a big purpose.

Sam stated that we could go rafting here in the swift waters. I told him I am from West Virginia. The New River Gorge in southern West Virginia is known worldwide for its white-water rafting. We agreed we did not have time that day but on our next trip there we would go rafting together.

We toured a small zoo that had animal naïve of the area. Then we found a place to sit where we could just enjoy the scenery.

Geofrey went down to the edge of the water to take walk. A few minutes later, I heard a big splash. Sam and I looked down to see Geofrey underwater being pulled by the rapid current. He was holding his cellphone up out of the water, as if to say, Save the cell phone! I threw down my purse immediately to prepare to get into the water to save him. My heart sunk as I ran toward the water. Sam was right behind me. We got to the edge of the swift water to see Geofrey fighting to make it to shore. Swinging his arms from side to side. His arm got close enough for us to reach him. We pulled him out of the water onto the rocky shore.

Geofrey let out a big cough and water came out of his mouth. Sam and I looked at each other with relief and then I looked at Geofrey in a way a mother does before she is about to correct their child.

"You almost gave me a heart attack, Geofrey! How can you worry about that cell phone? We can replace a cell phone but not you!" After I got my anger out, I then began to hug him. Thankful that he was safe.

Sam never said a word as he was drying Geofrey off with an extra shirt that he had brought with him. I am a nurse. I am trained to help people in emergency situations. Because it was Geofrey, it made it more emotional. After all he saved my life just a year earlier. After making sure he was stable, we decided that we had enough drama for the day. It was better for us to drive back to Entebbe where he could get a medial check-up.

I stayed close to him for the next 24 hours but by the next day he said he was feeling physically fine. But emotionally still shook up. We all still feeling a bit uneasy.

I had just a few more days left of my trip, but I wanted to meet Zaake Francis. The parliament member that I had seen be hit in the head by a chair on the floor of parliament. To me that scene was barbaric, but especially for government.

I think Sam was excited for this meeting because Zaake is a leader and a celebrity in Uganda. I wanted to talk to him about what life was like for children in the district in which he represented in government. We decided to meet at Pope Paul International Hotel in Kampala. As before I got into Sam's car and said, "It's just like an action movie."

To an American, talking about kidnapping and torture sounds like we are talking about something that happened in the past, like events from the Middle Ages. Since I had seen Zakke on television just a year earlier he had been kidnapped and tortured. The story sounded much like what I heard at Iddi Amin's torture chambers a few days earlier.

Compared to Las Vegas hotels, Pope Paul International Hotel was average on the inside. African style décor yet classy. Sam and I went toward that bar and sat at a table. We ordered food while we waited for Zaake to arrive. I ordered a hamburger and Sam ordered something that looked like African food trying to be American food. Just as we were finishing our dinner, Zaake came around the corner of the bar. My first thought was, He is much more attractive in person. He is a man of average height, round face, body is built round, a big, beautiful smile with a small dimple on his left cheek.

He was wearing the hat of his pollical party, People Power. It is a red beret with Uganda on it that says "People Power our power" on it. He friend Bobi Wine was the leader of this pollical party with the goal of changing things in their country. Of course, I heard stories of how it was dangerous to been seen wearing one of these hats. I was aware of the danger that came with sitting with Zaake Francis in public in Kampala.

We ordered more food and drinks to settle in to talk to Zaake about whatever he felt comfortable with telling us. Just like any other time with friends we were getting to know each other, laughing, and eating. Since I am passionate about helping children, Zaake showed me videos of the living conditions of some children in the Mityana Municipality which he represents as a member of parliament. The living conditions were worse than anything I had seen. A sense of sadness came over me for those children, but I could sense the determination in his voice to make a difference.

An hour later a man dressed in uniform approached the table from my right side. It did not startle me, after all when you go to the ATM in Uganda there are armed guards on both sides of you with AK-47s. It is common to see uniformed officers with weapons walking around especially in downtown Kampala. The man walked behind me and then to the left side of Zaake. I looked over at Sam. His smile turned to a look of concern. It was obvious that the man approaching the table was not one the good guys.

The gentleman stood there for a few moments in silence. By then we all had a look of concern on our faces. I was aware that sitting next to Zaake in Uganda was a risk. It was like if we were sitting next to Mandela in South Africa during the time when apartheid as a system was ruling. The man spoke to Zaake then put his hand out in a gesture to shake his hand. The looks of concern on our faces then turned to surprise—we had thought the man was coming to make trouble. Instead, he was coming to make peace. Zaake shook his hand. The gentleman identified himself as secret service agent of the Vice President of Uganda. He then pointed to the bar where a man was sitting having a drink. He did not say tell us who he was pointing to, but I assumed that was Edward Seekandi, the Vice President of Uganda.

The secret service officer said to Zaake, "We only bother you because we are ordered to do so. I urge you to continue." Then he quietly told us all to have a good night.

The heavy tension I was feeling began to release. I could see a look of relief on Sam's face. I let out an awkward laugh, to break the tension. I am known to tell jokes during inappropriate times like these. As the man walked away, I said out loud, "Well, I do not blame him for having a drink at the bar after work. If my boss was a dictator, I would want to have a drink after work too."

Sam and Zaake began to laugh out loud which broke the tension.

I then said, "I am from Las Vegas, we pay no mind to famous people drinking at bars. If he would not have pointed out the Vice President sitting there, I would have not known who he was."

About an hour after that encounter, Zaake decided to call it a night and return to his family. As Sam and I were getting into his car, I said, "I would have never thought when I saw that man on television in Minnesota that I would be sitting next to him in Uganda a year later. "Sam said, "Life is unpredictable. I never thought I would get to meet him either."

The tone in the car was one of sadness because I had just one more day in Uganda. But then it turned to teasing me about my date with a Prince. My only come back was that I was okay with him teasing me. But it must be nice to be in a relationship with someone special. I was not looking forward to all the things that come along with first dates. I think I would rather live through the dangers of the last couple of days then the awkward things about a first date.

We both laughed. Sam put in his Dolly Pardon music for the trip back.

Chapter 16:

A date with a Prince, Pizza in Milan and a plane trip home.

"There are two races of men in this world but only these two: the race of the decent man and the race of the indecent man."
-Viktor E. Frankl

Prince Fredrick called to tell me to meet me at the restaurant of my hotel at 6 pm. I was nervous, and I was not sure of what to wear. I had bought a dress in Entebbe a few days earlier, so I put that on. It was purple my favorite color. Fitting since I was going on a date with royalty.

During my time in Uganda, I was never treated different because I am a white American. Throughout my trip, I had the experience with the angry cab driver in Dubai. Ignorance can be found anywhere. What matters to me is the character of a person, not their race, culture, or economic status.

I must admit I still had trust issues with men. I had built a wall around myself as a protection. But not only was it protecting me it was also keeping people out.

When he showed up, he was dressed in a suit and tie. He is a handsome slender man, high cheek bones, even has the gait of a royal. He is the very image of his grandfather.

"Hello, Martha, how are you doing?" he said with a big smile so bright it could have light up the room.

"I am fine, Fredrick." I tried to match his big smile.

He pulled out my chair at the table of the dining area then sat right next to me. We exchanged pleasantries and then we looked at the menu. We began to compare American food with Ugandan

"Do you know what you want to have for dinner?" I closed my menu and stated I will have the fish and French fries. I forgot, here they are called chips. In the US, we call them French fries."

As the waitress was taking the menus, Fredrick leaned forward and put his hand on mine. "Enough about food. Tell me more about you."

I found this move to be a bit forward. I understood he was a man with influence that was probably the way he operates.

I looked at our hands touching on the table then looked up at Fredrick's face looking directly in my eyes. I thought to myself, I recognize that look, that is how I look at the gelato at the Venetian Hotel in Las Vegas.

With a look of embarrassment on my face I stuttered, "Hmm, what would you like to know?"

Fredrick said with that amazing smile, "Whatever you feel comfortable telling me." Just then he began to slowly lean in to kiss me. It was slow and gentle. Not rushed like a few days before at the palace. This time we were not interrupted. That kiss broke the tension between us.

After that, my shoulders began to relax, and we began to talk about our lives, our likes, and dislikes. Just like any other first date. Our food came, we laughed, and enjoyed each other's company until the restaurant was ready to close for the night. T

The waitress came around to say that they were closing for the night in an hour. I was used to Las Vegas where nothing closes, and I apologized for the inconvenience. The young lady stated, "It is fine, we are glad you enjoyed your dinner."

We paid the bill, then Fredrick stated he would call for a car home but first he was going to walk me to my hotel room before returning to Kampala.

It had been a long time since I had been single and on a first date. I had never been on a date with an African Prince. As we stood at my hotel door I felt like an awkward teenager. I kept thinking, What is the proper etiquette? Do I invite him in? What are the cultural norms here? My mind was filled with anxiety, and it showed on the outside. I awkwardly took out my keys to my hotel room from my purse and they fell in the floor.

Fredrick, being a gentleman, picked them up for me.

I said, "Thank you," as I opened the door. I looked at him while I was turning the key, and the thought in my mind was, He isn't leaving. Why is he still standing here?

Even an awkward teenager could answer that question. It was basic human nature and obvious as to why he was still standing there. But my anxiety was keeping me from seeing it. I asked him, "Would you like to come inside for a night cap? As you know I do not drink alcohol, but I do have some water and Coca-Cola."

Fredrick said with a smile, "Sure," as he entered the room.

He quickly made himself at home in the room, sitting on the side of the bed, which made me even more uncomfortable. I said, "Let me get that water for you." I came back with the water and as he reached for the bottle of water, he grabbed me and pulled me into the bed. He was a man of power, and he was going to get what he wanted.

The next morning, I woke up in Entebbe, Uganda, in bed with a tall dark and handsome Prince next to me. As I opened my eyes to see him sleeping next to me, it was almost like a dream. I just kept thinking; How on Earth did this happen? I still had some self-esteem issues left from the past. But what better way to get back into dating then to spend the night with a handsome African Prince.

As Prince Fredrick rose from the bed he said, "Good morning honey."

I just looked at him as if to say, who are you talking to?

He said, "I like the way you talk, the accent and how you call people darlin' and doll. I thought my nickname for you should be honey." I laughed. "Honey it is then."

We got dressed and walked back to the restaurant for breakfast. Fredrick pulled out his cell phone to call for a car home for two hours later. He said he had a meeting to attend that morning and he could not be late for it.

It was time for me to say good-bye to Uganda. Sam was on his way to pick me up and take me to the airport. I was sad that it was ending. But grateful that a new family was coming into my life. That I put myself out there and went on a date. A tall dark and handsome Prince was a pretty good way to get my groove back.

It was an emotional good-bye at the airport, almost as much as when I arrived. But I knew I would be back. That it was just the beginning. I was determined to help the children at Bulamu.

I had one more stop on before returning to Las Vegas. Pizza in Milan, to mark off everything on the list I had started my trip with.

Chapter 17:

2020 the year of the nurse. A pandemic nurse in a tourist town.

"In times of crisis, people reach for meaning. Meaning is strength. Our survival may depend on our seeking and finding it.
– Viktor E. Frankl

Just a few months after returning to Las Vegas the world changed by the Covid-19 pandemic. As a nurse, it meant the beginning of a battle with an enemy we knew little about. People dying all around me from an enemy that we could not see, and we had no weapons to use against it.

In the breakroom of the Emergency department in January 2020 was the first time I heard the word Covid-19. We were told that there was a pneumonia-type illness discovered in China. Las Vegas is one of the biggest tourist towns in the world. Forty million people visit from all over the world every year. My first thought was, "If there is a fast-spreading virus, it is a matter of time before it comes to Vegas."

It looked like your typical breakroom. Lockers, a small kitchen complete with a microwave that no one cleans, and tables for eating during breaks. Nurses sitting at tables wearing their fresh, clean scrubs ready to start their shift. As I looked around, I saw people drinking coffee, rubbing their eyes, and putting their stethoscopes around their necks preparing for the day ahead. We had our first meeting about policies. We were given guidelines of who to quarantine. That day it was people who had been to China in the last sixty days who presented with a fever and respiratory symptoms. I still remember the look on the charge nurse's face that morning. A look of fear and exhaustion as she rubbed her forehead. Mumbling as though she was trying to find the right words. The guidelines that were given to us changed daily from then on out.

Just two months later, the horrors that we were seeing daily can only be described as something from a Stephen King novel. People were coming to the hospital with mild symptoms by the end of the twelve hour shift we would be calling their time of death.

Caring for the sick, that is what nurses do. That means putting ourselves in harm's way. There are people to be cared for, no matter what the illness may be. Conspiracy theories still abound about Covid-19. Where it came from, whether there was something nefarious going on, and whether the vaccine is safe. As a nurse, I did not have time to argue or debate with people about my opinion on these issues. Inside the hospital we were trying to keep people alive. Keep ourselves safe as well.

I had many years of experience as a nurse when the Pandemic came. As a new nurse I had pandemic training. The information was from the Spanish Flu in 1918. When I attended that training, I thought that I would have to use it. Nothing could have prepared me for being a nurse in 2020.

Daily life as a nurse in a tourist town is much the same as being a nurse anywhere else. Except you have people coming from all over the world to your town for vacation. I describe Las Vegas as the Disneyland for adults. Never a shortage of people coming in the Emergency Department with what you might call "interesting" injuries. My favorite are the people who look very innocent yet when they come to triage it is a different story.

For example, a short bald man that looked as though his age was in his seventies. At first glance he looked like an innocent grandpa. He walked up to me one morning as I was working the triage area, he shouted, "Hey nurse I am from Little Rock, Arkansas. Do you want to know what I did last night?" with a grin so big it covered his entire face. As he stood in front of the nurse's station, he was swaying around and slurring his words.

As a nurse I politely escorted him to an examine room with the response of, "No sir, I do not want to know what you did last night. But I know whatever you did, it is not legal in Arkansas." A sense of humor really helps when you are a nurse especially in a tourist town.

Sights and sounds of the emergency department are just what you might think: ambulance sirens, coughing, screaming, bleeding, crying, Stroke calls, and Code blues. All of what I like to call organized chaos. I have worked many disciplines within nursing, but the Emergency room was always my favorite. I like to be able to help people right away and send them on to where they need to go to get better. Its only downside is that you don't get to see what happens to them later. But I always feel blessed to be there for people when they need someone the most.

Nasal passage swabs became something that was talked about in the media. In Healthcare, we have always done them. In the ER, swabbing the nose for MRSA is common. I guess to a non-medical person, it does seem like a strange thing to do. I like to put people at ease with my sense of humor. After I explain what I am about to do, I tell a joke as I am about to swab their nose. I say, "Remember when we were children and we used to say, you can pick your nose, but you can't pick your friend's nose? Well, my friend, I am about to pick your nose." If someone has any sense of humor they laugh or sometimes they look at me like, as if I am crazy. But it usually works because the NP swab is done and over before they know it.

Policies changed daily. Masks became mandatory. Screening stations were established at the hospital entrances. Taking temperatures and asking about respiratory symptoms of people before they entered the hospital. By mid-March it was declared an official pandemic.

The first patient that I took care of with suspected Covid will always stand out in my mind. She was an elderly lady. She came to the hospital complaining of shortness of breath and fever. We put her in on air borne precaution room. Put supplemental oxygen on her. I was dressed head to toe in protective gear. As she was lying there just a glance at face you could see she was afraid.

Because she could not have family or friends visit, staff were her only companions. As I was caring for her, she looked at me and said, "Today would have been Elvis's birthday."

I stopped what I was doing. "Really? Wonder how old he would have been today?"

She said, "I am not sure, but I loved his music in my younger days. This is Las Vegas, and he was the King of Rock and Roll," she said with a smile. "Would you sing an Elvis song to me?"

My first job was singing telegrams a long time ago. But when a lady that is that sick and afraid asks you to sing Elvis. You sing Elvis.

The sound of an off-key version of "Now or Never" by Elvis Presley could be heard from the hallway. The protective gear that I was wearing made it sound more muffled. The king of rock and roll would have probably turned in his grave at the sound of it. But it made her happy and that's what mattered.

By March 2020, it had been declared a pandemic and Las Vegas went on lockdown. As a nurse, I had a pass to be out on the streets. One morning in mid-March I found myself standing on Las Vegas Boulevard by myself. Las Vegas Boulevard also known as the Vegas strip. It is a famous strip of land that is the home to landmarks and hotels that make Las Vegas, Vegas. The sidewalks are usually filled with people, elbow to elbow. Happy smiling tourists that come to experience the Disneyland for adults or "Sin City."

The strip always looks alive, it's a constant party. Bright lights, music, and happy couples walking hand and hand. One morning around 5 am on my way to work, I looked around as I sat in my car at the stop light in front of the Wynn Hotel. I noticed that I was the only person on the strip.

I started to freak out at the thought I was the only person on Las Vegas Boulevard. I keep looking around for other cars and people. It looked like a scene from the movie the day the Earth stood still. A town that looks alive 24/7 was now deserted. I pulled over when I could. I thought who I can call? It was 5 am and everyone I knew was either still in bed, or at work. But someone else had to see this.

I called my friend Sam in Uganda. I called him and said, "Sam you are never going to believe this, I am alone on Las Vegas Boulevard. When will this every happen again?" Then I sent him a video of what I was seeing.

I felt like I was grieving the loss of a loved one. It was a city that I had come to love. I will always consider myself a Vegas girl no matter where in the world I am located. Through the grieving and shock of what I was seeing, I knew this was historical. Since I would never be alone on the strip again, I should do something that I will never get to do. I will tell on myself; I broke a traffic law. I did an illegal turn in the middle of Las Vegas Boulevard that morning.

At the end of March 2020, there was a confirmed case of Covid-19 in a homeless shelter in Las Vegas. In Vegas there is an underground city of homeless people. Underneath the bright lights and happy vacationing tourists filling the sidewalks is an entirely different world. Homeless people from all walks of life, driven underground because tourists would not fill the streets if the streets were lined with homeless people. The Vegas underground had begun to be infected with Covid.

That's when I went to work at the field hospital in downtown Las Vegas. When I interviewed, I was asked if I would be afraid to go into the underground. I replied, "Nurses take care of people, all people regardless of race, culture, or economic status."

My first day on the job, I was instructed to park my car out front of the first tent, then report in there where further instructions would be given. Once I had signed in and proved my identity, I was instructed to go to the dressing area. That was where we would shower and don our protective gear. The young lady who was giving me instructions pointed to a locker where I could put my personal belongings. She then pointed to the tent behind that one to say that is where I would be doffing my protective gear.

After putting on the required protection, I was directed to an area between the tents. A group of nurses and doctors stood there waiting for instructions. We were told what each tent was used for and what tasks we were to perform during our shift. It was the same type of meeting I attended before my shift in the ER break room just a couple of months earlier, but this one was much different. Back then we did not know when Covid-19 was coming to town. Now I was standing in the middle of it. In a temporary hospital downtown Las Vegas. Ready to fight the devil that had the world locked in fear.

Just a few shifts into my time at the field hospital we started to see patients with covid-like symptoms. People were quickly going south. It was becoming more frequent that we had to transfer patients to the Emergency Department of a nearby hospital. I was springtime in the Nevada desert, and we were wearing full protective gear. We had to protect ourselves from Covid and dehydration. Our management took good care of us. We always had plenty of water and snacks.

Each tent inside had small, partitioned hospital rooms, with a small cot inside each one for the patient to lay on. We had supplies to take vital signs, treat wounds, and give supplemental oxygen. Any more complicated than that we had to send them out. Mostly it was people living in the underground system of Las Vegas coming to us to with respiratory symptoms to be tested for Covid-19.

On one particularly difficult day, a co-worker and I stepped out of a tent after caring for a patient. We were heading to the break tent for some water. I have a way with showing my sense of humor at what some might consider the wrong times. I look at her and said,

"I don't know about you, but I am tired of living in a historical event." I couldn't see her under all the protective gear, but I could hear her laugh. We took a selfie at that moment. Then we walked to the break tent side by side. In a way, we were almost holding each other up. It was a long shift under all that protective gear and the Nevada sun was beating straight down on us.

On the right at the field hospital downtown Las Vegas in 2020.

I was picking up shifts at the field hospital in downtown Las Vegas and working in the emergency department at a hospital near the Las Vegas Strip. People were quarantined in their homes, but I was going straight into the very thing the entire world was afraid of.

Daily life had changed for all. But for me it felt like I was living the movie Contagion. Entire units of the hospital were now turned into Covid wards.

There are a few shifts that will always be on my mind. A mother and son who both had Covid-19 were dying in two different rooms just feet from each other in the ICU. I had to call a young lady and tell her that her mother and brother both were at the end of their lives. Not an easy call for me to make, and I can't even imagine how that young lady felt to receive that call.

The second was a particularly difficult shift in the ICU. An hour before my twelve-hour shift was ending, I was helping a priest don his protective gear for the fifth time in that shift. He was giving last rights to a patient. I wanted to help him don and doff his protective gear because I knew he did not know how to do it properly. I did not want him to be exposed.

As I was helping him on that fifth time in twelve hours, I looked him in the eyes and said, "Well, padre, I think we are friends now."

He gave me a smile through his mask. He then said, "I hope we get to meet again under different circumstances." After what we had witnessed together that day, we had forged a bond.

The way we did things as nurses had to be changed to accommodate. Outside the patients' rooms were stations with Personal Protective gear in them. Before going into a room, we had to stand in front of the PPE station to don and doff the equipment properly. Which made response time to call lights longer. Not much we could do about it because we had to protect ourselves. I stood at that changing station saying in my head and sometimes out loud, "This is the worst wardrobe change ever." It was poor timing for jokes but sometimes jokes help us get through the difficult times. We wore scrubs, then an isolation gown, an N95 respirator, a cap on our heads, a shield to protect our eyes and if we were lucky, we had a PAPR, Powered air-purifying respirator.

Taking off the PPE was just as big a chore as putting it on. Taking off the PPE in the proper order was important so that we did not expose ourselves to the virus. That increased our time away from caring for the patients. We were constantly running out of supplies.

One shift a lab employee discovered we were out of isolation gowns, and it was going to take a while for the charge nurse to get more. He said, "I have to go in and draw these labs." Then I saw him go down the hall. He came back wearing a trash bag that he had neatly cut to look just like an isolation gown. I was impressed at his creativity, and I would hire that guy. That was problem solving skills at its finest.

We had to become creative and find new ways to do things. Because no one could have visitors, we started to use facetime and video chats to keep people in contact with their loved ones. People who had been married thirty to forty years were saying goodbye to their spouses over video chat. The way people went through the grieving process had changed and we had to find ways to assist them.

The world was on hold, while the world stayed at home, I felt like I was going into war to battle an enemy we could not see and had little to use to fight against it.

Chapter 18:

A weekend in Vegas with a Prince.

"Happiness cannot be pursued; it must ensue."
-Viktor E. Frankl

I still had the purpose of helping the children at Bulamu. With the world at a standstill, working as a nurse during the pandemic so that goal was put on hold. I kept in touch with my Ugandan family daily. Prince Fredrick introduced me to his cousin Prince Mwana that was living in California. He was writing about the Kingdom and was talking about writing a book about Edward Mutesa. He thought I might find it interesting to talk to him. He is a doctor, so we would have working in the healthcare field in common as well.

Just before the lock down came in Las Vegas I invited Prince Mwanga to visit me. He said he had never visited Las Vegas and I thought we would enjoy spending some time together. I knew that Las Vegas would be a culture shock for him the way Uganda was for me. But I had toured much of Vegas during my time there so he would be getting a good guide of the city.

I knew I had to push on and date again. It was the beginning of tearing down the wall I had built around myself and letting people in. I had made new friends in Vegas. I was a social person. The past taught me what I wanted and did not want in a relationship. I was really to move forward and date, but I was going to do it cautiously even if my date was a Prince.

I picked Prince Mwanga up at the airport. He was wearing blue jeans and a nice button-up dress shirt. A handsome man, very slender, small build and shorter than me. Soft-spoken with a British accent. From our phone conversations I can the impression that he was much different than Prince Fredrick. A quiet, shy, conservative gentleman.

As I greeted him, we exchanged pleasantries, he immediately pointed out, "There are gambling machines in the airport" with a surprised look on his face. I said, "Welcome to Las Vegas Prince Mwanga. Darlin just to let you know, there are gambling machines everywhere here." As I guided him to my car, I realized that this weekend was going to be like living a real-life version of the movie 'Coming to America.'

After picking him up at the airport, we then drove to Las Vegas Boulevard. I wanted him to see all the iconic sights of Las Vegas that I could fit into one weekend. Caesar's palace, the Bellagio fountains, the volcano at the Mirage, and my favorite—the Venetian Hotel. As we drove through the bright lights Prince Mwanga was silent. I asked him if he was feeling alright. When I glanced over at him, I noticed a big grin on his face. I enjoyed seeing the reaction on his face just from the sights of the beautiful buildings of Vegas. It is all over the top, which I love.

After he got settled into his hotel room, our first stop was the Venetian Hotel. A beautiful hotel that is modeled after the Venice, Italy. We were engaging in small talk as we walked to where you board the gondolas. Suddenly he stopped mid-sentence and his body went still. A lady walked by us in a revealing two-piece show girl outfit with a see-through wrap around her.

He said, "Oh my, did you see that black American she was almost naked!" as he grabbed his chest in a display that seemed a bit over the top.

"Calm down that is a Vegas show girl." Then I began to laugh.

"Someone should call her father. How can she be dressed that way in public?" Prince Mwanga said as he was still holding his chest.

I started to lead him to the entrance to the gondola ride. "I understand your reaction. That's how I felt when I saw the traffic in Uganda the first time. Let take a ride on the gondolas I think you will enjoy it."

We ended the evening in the replica of Saint Mark's Square eating gelato. We agreed we should call it an early evening. We had a full schedule the next few days.

The next morning, we decided to start our day together by meeting for breakfast. My favorite breakfast place in Vegas as a view of the strip across the street from the Mirage Hotel. The sight of the working volcano and the waterfall in front is relaxing.

We spend the morning talking about our experiences working in hospitals. Comparing Uganda to the United States. He told me about Edward Mutesa's exile from Mengo palace. I shared a part of my story with him. At this point, I had built a good friendship with many within the Buganda Kingdom. I know that might sound a bit farfetched coming from a Las Vegas lady, with a southern accent. I had come to respect the current reigning King, Ronald Mutebi. So much so that I went to leadership in the United States to advocate for him.

Next, we set off for an action fill day. The Bellagio fountains, Caesar's palace and to the top of the Eiffel tower at the Paris Hotel. Watching Prince Mwanga see Las Vegas for the first time was like I was seeing it again for the first time. The wonder and excitement in his face when he first saw the Bellagio Fountain show made it seem magical.

His reactions went between amazement and shock. When walking along the strip I avoided the people handing out cards advertising "escort services" based on his reaction to a Vegas showgirl outfit I did not think he could handle it. The constant activity and the streets filled with people. In Uganda things close early in the evening. Walking with an open container of alcohol and the smell of marijuana were the two things I believe he had the biggest reaction to during his trip. When I told him that Vegas has stores that just sell marijuana, he did not believe it, so I drove him to one to show him.

When I dropped him off at the airport, I knew this the beginning of a relationship. The first one since I left the toxic situation in West Virginia. During my time there, I was told how awful I was, how I was no good, that I was unworthy almost daily. I bought into it. Now I knew it wasn't true. I was worthy enough to be at the side of a Prince.

After that we began to go back and forth between Los Angeles where he lived and Las Vegas. We had many things in common. In the ways that he was different than me, we balanced each other. We were moving forward, and I was beginning to take down the wall that I had put around myself for protection.

Chapter 19:

Surviving Covid.

"Man's inner strength may raise him above his outward fate."
-Viktor E. Frankl

One morning I was getting ready for work, standing at the sink brushing my teeth doing my daily routine. I started to feel lightheaded. The room began to spin. I placed myself on the floor, then began to crawl and feel my way to my bed. I lived alone so the only thing to do was to call for help. It was difficult to see the phone to call for help. My cell phone looked as though it was spinning, the numbers were all mixed up. I kept closing my eyes and then re-opening them to see the numbers more clearly. I went from being the nurse caring for patients with Covid to being one of the patients. I was now one of the people laying on a gurney in the hallway of the emergency room.

As I lay on the gurney in the emergency room in the hallway, I was having difficulty breathing. I knew it was Covid before they told me. I had seen it over the past few months. I knew what the devil we were all afraid of looked like. I was afraid, but not of dying. I had been through a lot in my life. I was afraid I would die and not finish what I set out to do in life, help the orphans in Uganda.

I had been the patient many times in the past. Now I was seeing what Covid patients had seen as I was busy in the ER. My lungs felt tight, breathing was difficult. Every inch of my body ached. I had supplemental oxygen. All my attention was on breathing. My fever spiked to over 101, the chills were so strong that my body was shaking all over. My fellow nurses gave me medication and put ice packs behind my neck and under my arm pits to decrease my body temperature. Then she asked me if I had any family that she could call for me.

My family had turned away from me, so the answer was no. But Kelly, my best friend in Las Vegas, was my emergency contact. Kelly and I became friends when she first moved to Vegas from Florida a year earlier. We are alike in many ways in that we like the same movies, food, and many things on the Las Vegas strip. When you meet her, you might think she is the outgoing party girl. The color of her hair changes frequently. Pink, green, purple hair with spikes on the top with colorful outfits to match. I am the outgoing social person, and she is the introvert who likes to stay at home curled up on the couch with her cat. The nurse stated she would call Kelly and let her know that I was in the hospital.

About an hour later my nurse came back to say she spoke to Kelly's son and that my best friend was in the hospital with Covid as well. I was at battle with the enemy but this time a patient. Because it was difficult to breath I laid still. I tried to keep my mind occupied. I thought about all the happy things I could. While in the background my co-workers fought the enemy as nurses and doctors. The sight of seeing people dying of Covid around you as you lay there makes you feel helpless. Especially when you are used to being the caregiver.

As I was wheeled to my hospital room, I looked at the PPE stations outside the rooms as I was lying flat on the gurney. The worst wardrobe change ever, I thought in my mind. I was moved over in my bed. I looked up at the ceiling. It was a view I was familiar with from my car accident some years earlier.

After the car accident in West Virginia, I was left with only a view of the ceiling in my hospital room. In Las Vegas in 2020 that was my view once again. I knew I was not going to ask my nurse to sing Elvis like I had done for a patient. But I did feel that I was being well cared for. After all, I knew what it was like to the nurse in this situation.

Days in the hospital of looking at that ceiling, struggling to breathe. Each day got easier. Going to the bathroom on my own for the first time felt like the biggest milestone. When you walk your oxygen demand rises. Just that walk to the bathroom left me feeling exhausted. I lost weight fast. The weight I had gained from sitting at home eating during lockdown was gone and then some. I am five foot six inches tall. When I left the hospital, I was 117 pounds. My face was sunken in and my body weak and frail. But I was still here. When I was wheeled out of the hospital, I was grateful to see the beauty of a Nevada sunset. On the way home, I kept teasing my friend Kelly that we needed to get matching T-shirts that said, "We kicked Covid's ass."

I moved in with Kelly in her apartment. That way we would both have the support of a friend, share the expenses. The goal that I had when I first moved to Las Vegas two years earlier was finally coming true. We were two single ladies living just minutes from the Las Vegas strip. I was still dating Prince Mwanga, with the quarantine in effect it was difficult for anyone to see each other. That when I used Facetime and all the things, I helped my patients use to keep in touch with their loved ones.

At this point it felt like the past few years I had lived a decade. The experiences made me strong and wiser. I was a different person then when I left my home with just a suitcase just a few years earlier. When a look who I was when I was sitting on that bench at the Minneapolis Airport, I do not recognize that person. She looked hollow inside, with messy appearance. Like a shell of a human being.

After all the experiences, I was now the butterfly that was emerging from its cocoon. I think it was me discovering who I was. I still had one more thing to accomplish, help the children. Once the pandemic was over, I knew I was going to get to work on it.

Within me I still had one more thing that was lingering, making peace with what I had lived in West Virginia.

Chapter 20:

Take me home country roads.

"Even when it is not fully attained, we become better by striving for a higher goal."
-Viktor E. Frankl

Once the covid cases had dropped in number and travel was allow again I boarded a plane at McCarran International Airport in Las Vegas. The end destination was Charleston, West Virginia where I left my life behind with only a suitcase just four years earlier.

I had anxiety about returning. Many attempts to make amends with my parents had failed. I was not sure how they would react when I came to their door. It was what I needed to have closure.

As I heard the pilot announce that we would be landing in fifteen minutes at Yeager Airport, my heart sank. I started to think how I could be coming back to the place that I had to run from. The place that did not want me. I had been bullied, abused, and my cries for help had been ignored. It took my Ugandan family from far away to help me. As I looked around at the rest of the passengers a flash of what I had experienced came into my mind.

I was exiled from West Virginia but now I belong to the world.

As I walked to rental car counter to the right was a television screen playing country roads by John Denver on a loop. Throughout my journey when people found out that I was originally from West Virginia they would break out into song. "Take me home, country roads, to the place I belong, West Virginia, mountain momma," was usually the only lyrics they could remember. John Denver really got around. The ladies working the rental car counter had to listen to him for hours.

After renting the car I took a picture of that suitcase at the airport. As a symbol that it had come home. It had seen a lot in four years. If it could talk it could tell one helluva story. I decided to meet up with my friend Debbie. Of all the people I knew for years she and I stayed close.

I booked a room at the only casino in Charleston, West Virginia. After all, I was a Las Vegas girl now. As you can imagine it is not like the Venetian or Caesar's place. Just a small hotel outside of town. Charleston is the state Capital. When I lived there seeing the beauty of the gold dome of the state capital always made me smile. I planned a trip to the Capital building the next morning along with driving to all the places where I had experienced horrors in my life.

After a night of rest, the next morning I drove to the State Capital Building first. A way to start the day in a positive way. I graduated nursing school at the University of Charleston just across the river from the state capital. I stood on the porch of the state capital building and gazed at my alumni mater. Sixteen years before I had walked that stage in my cap and gown. I was eager to be a nurse and ready to help the world. In a sense, I guess I ended up doing that.

After I walked the grounds of the capital building, I got into my car and drove to the house I ran from with that suitcase. As I drove up to the house, I did not go near it because a lovely young couple now own the house. The memory of the horror of this place playing in my mind for the last four years as though it was this big scary place. As I stood in front of it seemed so small and unimportant.

When I left, I had stood at the end of the porch, looked my then husband in the eyes stated, "You will never see my face again."

That is a promise I had kept good on. It was like at that moment I had taken back my power. It was the moment I had said, I'd had enough.

I wiped the tears from my eyes, said a little prayer and got in my car. It was time to visit the house that my ex and I built together. When I was in the car accident, we had just finished building a house. We had built it with our hands. Took us years to build and it was something we were both proud of.

West Virginia roads are winding, narrow and not always paved. Where we had chosen to build our house was on a classic West Virginia Road. It is on top of a steep hill, outside of town. It was always quiet. When I was there alone, I had a lot of peace.

I got out of my car in front of the house. It was like I was standing looking at the past. It was healing, and I began to cry. Tears of joy and pain. Tears of happiness.

I made it.

I not only survived, but I thrived. I traveled the world with that suitcase, I did amazing things and met incredible people. I was standing looking at the past and hopeful for the probabilities of the future. I stood there sobbing for what was a few minutes but felt like longer. I thought it was time to go spend time with my friends. End my day on a positive note. The next morning was going to be the most difficult part of my trip. I was driving to my parents' house.

The next morning, I got up early to drive the two hours to my parents' house. I grew up in Fairmont, West Virginia. The drive itself brought back memories of all the times my ex and I had driven to visit our families. The state slogan is Wild, Wonderful West Virginia. The scenery on my drive was beautiful. I love the Nevada desert, but I missed trees and green grass at times. That drive was full of rolling green hills and lots of green trees. When I pulled into town, I got flashes of my high school days. East Fairmont High School, such a small place but wonderful memories.

I was just two blocks away from my parent's house when I panicked. I could not knock on that door yet. Fairmont is famous for two things—hot dogs and pepperoni rolls. It had been over four years since I had either. I pulled into a little hot dog place on the across from East Fairmont High School and had both. After all it had been four years. Just like all those years before they did not disappoint. They were just as delicious as they always were.

The pictures on the walls of the East Fairmont High School students in their football and basketball uniforms reminded me of when my friend Vanessa and I joined the basketball team. We reconnected in Minneapolis. We still laugh about that time all these year later. We say to one another, "Remember when we thought it was a good idea to join the basketball team?" Then we laugh. It seemed like a more innocent time. Maybe it was, or it was just that we were young and had not experienced the world yet. Most likely it was a little of both.

I finally got the courage to park across the street from my parents' house. I took a deep breath as if to help build up my courage from the driver's seat. I don't know why this was difficult for me. In the past four years I had traveled the world by myself. I had walked with royalty, seen, and done things most people had not with just a suitcase as my only possession. After building up the courage I walked up to the door and knocked. Then nothing happened. I knocked again. I thought, all this nervousness with the anticipation and traveling all the way here from Las Vegas, and they are not even here.

I thought I will knock one more time. This time the door opened, and it was my brother. My brother John was much other than me. We look nothing alike. He is tall, over six-foot, heavy-set man. We never had much of a relationship. This was the first time I had seen him since 2015. He did not show any emotion, as he opened the door slowly.

He said, "Dad has been sick for a while, and I came to help Mom care for him." My heart felt heavy. I am their daughter, and I am a nurse. Then that feeling of compassion left as quickly as it came.

As I stepped in the living room my father was sitting in a big chair with oxygen on. He looked frail and weak. I knew what was going on, COPD. He had been a smoker since he was seven years old. He was now almost eighty years old. These things catch up with you in time.

He then looked up at me. "You sure have gained some weight and you are blocking me from seeing the television."

That's when my feelings of compassion for him melted away. I was his daughter who had run for her life four years earlier and who he had not seen since. My mother came from the kitchen. I had heard she has cancer. In a small-town people talk. I did not receive a better welcome from her. I sat down on the couch next to my parents. I tried to explain to them why I was there. I was there to make peace. I guess people must have peace within themselves before they can be at peace with others. I stayed long enough to figure out that I was wasting my time. I left with small pleasantries and walked to my rental car across the street.

I sat in my car for a while to process what I had just experienced. It was like I had just been in the Twilight Zone. I had been deeply hurt by their rejection. But now I realized I was not the person I was four years ago. I did not need their validation. When you know who you are the approval of others is not needed. But I understood what it must orphans must feel at the orphanage to have place to call home and no one to turn to.

The next morning in the middle of packing my suitcase, I started to take everything out of it.

My friend Debbie said, "What on earth are you doing?" in her southern accent.

I said, "It is time to put the suitcase to rest."

She said with a confused look on her face, "Well, that's fine but you still have a plane to catch, and you need a suitcase."

"I will stop on the way to the airport and buy a new one." I said with a grin.

She said, "Fine, just get moving."

I dumped that suitcase in her trash at the end of her driveway on the way to the airport. It was symbolic that my journey was over. I was no longer that abused shell of a person I was when I had left just four years earlier. I had become the person I was meant to be. It was time to start helping the children. I boarded that plane at Chuck Yeager Airport to Las Vegas, Nevada as 'Mother Martha.'

That is how a nurse from West Virginia became know as 'Mother Martha' in Uganda.

www.ingramcontent.com/pod-product-compliance
Lightning Source LLC
Chambersburg PA
CBHW072058110526

44590CB00018B/3229